45]

The Human Shape of Work

The Human
Shape of Work

STUDIES IN THE SOCIOLOGY OF OCCUPATIONS

Edited by Peter L. Berger

PETER L. BERGER

ELY CHINOY

WILLIAM M. EVAN

RAYMOND L. GOLD

IAN LEWIS

KENNETH UNDERWOOD

THE MACMILLAN COMPANY, NEW YORK
COLLIER-MACMILLAN LIMITED, LONDON

Acknowledgment is hereby made to The American Society for
Engineering Education for permission to quote, in William F.
Evan's article, "On the Margin—The Engineering Technician,"
from the *Journal of Engineering Education*, Volume 48, No. 10
(June 1958), page 880.

First Printing

The Macmillan Company, New York

Collier-Macmillan Canada Ltd., Toronto, Ontario

Library of Congress catalog card number: 64-12541

Printed in the United States of America

CONTENTS

[v]

PREFACE

The present volume is conceived as a contribution to the sociology of work. Most of the contributors are sociologists, and all the contributions are placed in a sociological frame of reference. But it is assumed that the problem of these studies is of much broader interest. Consequently, technical sociological language has been avoided as much as possible. One important consequence of this frame of reference, however, is that it is analytic rather than prescriptive. We have sought to convey our understanding of these matters. We have not tried to offer any solutions.

A word about the contributors is in order. Raymond Gold teaches sociology at Montana State University. Ely Chinoy is professor and chairman of the Sociology Department at Smith College. William M. Evan is on the faculty of the School of Industrial Management at the Massachusetts Institute of Technology. Ian Lewis is an independent marketing consultant. Kenneth Underwood is on the faculty of Wesleyan University, where he directed its Institute of Ethics and Politics. Peter L. Berger is on the Graduate Faculty of the New School for Social Research, and is also connected with the Hartford Seminary Foundation.

A special word of thanks is due to Clement Alexandre, of The Macmillan Company, who originally conceived the idea of this volume, and patiently nurtured it to its realization. Thanks are also due to Lillian Jockheck for editorial assistance, and to the Hartford Seminary Foundation for putting various facilities at the disposal of the editor.

P. L. B.

THE
HUMAN SHAPE
OF WORK

STUDIES IN THE SOCIOLOGY OF OCCUPATIONS

I

In the Basement — The Apartment-Building Janitor*

RAYMOND L. GOLD

ANYONE WHO has lived in a big city in the United States knows something about apartment-building janitors. Hardly a day passes without some kind of interaction between the janitor and all his tenants. At the very least, the daily trip to the garbage pail or incinerator reminds tenants and janitor of each other. Their lives as urbanites are unavoidably bound up together.

This chapter is a story *about* and *by* the big-city apartment-building janitor: I tell it both in my words and in his. My general aim is to show how being in daily, interdependent relationships with tenants shapes him, and how he, in turn, attempts to shape these relationships. The narration is constructed of the several interrelated themes that account for

---

* This report is based upon a study of apartment-building janitors in Chicago that I made in 1949 and 1950. A complete report of the study is in Raymond L. Gold, "The Chicago Flat Janitor," unpublished M.A. thesis, University of Chicago, 1950.

the person and the interactions of the janitor. These themes concern work relationships—those with tenants, but also those with fellow janitors, bosses, and union officials. They concern mutual influences between the janitor's work behavior and self-conceptions, and between his personal and occupational aspirations. And, consistent with the central thesis of this book, they concern the human and moral tensions that develop in his work relationships. How the janitor struggles to live with these tensions is essentially the story of how many American urbanites struggle to live with the countless uncertainties, dilemmas, and frustrations of our society.

THE JOB

Lest there be some misunderstanding of the kind of janitorial work I am referring to, let me introduce the narration with a description of the apartment-building janitor's work situation, duties, responsibilities, and related matters. All the janitors I am discussing work solely in residential buildings in Chicago. They ordinarily work in one or more buildings by themselves, except that they may have helpers when working in a building that is too large to be serviced by one man. Janitors refer to the buildings they work in as the "job." This term may refer either to one or to all their buildings.

Most janitors work in buildings that consist of unfurnished apartments. In these buildings the janitor is the only permanent employee. The management provides no daily services for tenants other than those the janitor performs. Other janitors work in apartment hotels and hotels, both of which are usually staffed by a resident manager, desk clerks, switchboard operators, maids, and handymen. Ordinarily, these dwellings are furnished. Still other janitors work in cooperative buildings, where tenants own their apartments. Here, the janitor is again usually the only permanent employee; but, since tenants own their apartments, he may meet with servicing situations not found in ordinary flat buildings.

Apartment-building janitors in Chicago work exclusively in residential buildings that are heated by low-pressure steam (or hot-water) systems. Residential buildings utilizing high-pressure systems (that is, more than ten pounds of steam) are required by law to employ licensed stationary engineers. All nonresidential buildings are outside the janitor's domain.

The technical skills that janitors need master are few and simple. Much of their work requires no particular mechanical knowledge, while mastery of the remainder of their work requires only a few weeks' training on the job. Janitors are keenly aware of this. They are always eager to increase the relative importance of their mechanical work as compared to that of their nonmechanical work. They do this in two ways: verbally, by exaggerating their mechanical ability and deeds; and actually, by trying to learn esoteric skills of building tradesmen that would be useful to them.

The janitor is expected to know what to do in the event of an emergency. An emergency occurs in dramatic form when something suddenly goes wrong with the heating system, or with any other system vital to servicing the building; but usually it occurs in the form of a slowly leaking water pipe or faucet. Following the general principle of calling an appropriate building tradesman to correct major mechanical difficulties and of correcting minor ones himself, the janitor would shut off the water and call a plumber if a water pipe sprang a leak. He would repair a simple leak in a water faucet, but call a plumber to replace it were he to decide that the faucet is beyond repair. Repair of a faucet generally entails no more than shutting off the water and replacing a worn-out washer inside the faucet. His claim of an emergency allows him to do faucet-repair work, which is supposedly plumbers' work. So successfully have janitors exercised this claim that plumbers have come to identify faucet repairing with janitoring. It is now almost impossible to get plumbers to repair a faucet. They will gladly replace a leaking faucet, but are loath to repair one. To them, repairing faucets has become "janitors' work." But to janitors, faucet repairing has become an important symbol of growth in their stature as mechanics. When they talk glibly about repair jobs, they are actually saying that they are doing such things as repairing faucets. Casual and frequent mention of "repair jobs" seems to them to sound more impressive—almost as though they were building tradesmen talking about *their* repair work. Some janitors even go so far as to deplore the actions of colleagues "that overstep their bounds on repair work." Janitors who express this view are clearly implying that they could do such work too but that it would be unethical if they did.

Whenever they can, janitors watch building tradesmen at work in their buildings in order to increase their mechanical knowledge. Over a period of years, an observant janitor can thus acquire a useful array of remedies for the mechanical troubles that commonly occur in residential buildings. As will be shown shortly, the ability to do more than the required technical work may contribute importantly to establishing job security.

The janitor performs some work activities daily, some weekly, and some seasonally. He arises at about five-thirty in the morning to fire the furnace for heat in cold weather or for hot water in warm weather. Then he removes the tenants' garbage to the boiler room, where he burns it in the furnace. He does all this before many of the tenants are awake. During cold weather he has much coal to shovel during the course of the day. In warm weather he shovels into the furnace only enough coal to provide hot water. At about nine o'clock he eats breakfast, after which he begins the work that he customarily does on that day of the week. One day of the week is set aside for vacuuming halls, another for dusting, another for mopping the vestibules, another for polishing the brass and washing the windows in halls and vestibules, and so on. Some time is spent almost every day doing scheduled repair jobs for tenants. In the winter there is often snow to shovel, as well as coal, both of which consume much time and energy. Spring means putting in screens throughout the buildings he serves. It also means preparing the lawns for the summer. In summer lawns must be watered almost daily, but the heavy work of providing heat and removing snow is past, and so the summer months make relatively moderate demands on him. Autumn is the season when screens are removed and stored. It is also the time for raking and burning leaves. And it is the beginning of the long period during which the janitor must provide heat.

The length of the workday depends upon the season and the type of firing equipment the buildings have. In cold weather the workday begins at about five-thirty in the morning and ends at about nine-thirty at night. During especially cold weather, the janitor may start his fires somewhat earlier in the morning and bank them quite late at night. If his buildings are equipped with an automatic firing system (stoker or oil), his cold-weather workday is not shortened appreciably, but he spends much less time tending his fires during the day. In addition, he can push a lever to start the fires on Sunday and go back to bed, since he does not remove garbage on Sunday. During warm weather firing begins later and ends earlier, since it is only for hot water. With automatic firing the furnace needs almost no attention during the day, whereas hand-fired furnaces require two or three visits.

The amount of work done per day is small in relation to the length of the workday. The heavy work of shoveling coal and removing garbage takes two to four hours. Cleaning activities take about as much time, but not nearly so much effort. The variables, such as repair jobs and snow removal, account for another hour on the average, leaving six to eight hours of free time in the course of the workday. During this free time the janitor eats his meals, takes a nap, and finds ways of passing time as pleasantly as he can. This time is spent in the neighborhood because, firing duties notwithstanding, he must be available at all times in case of an emergency.

A NERVE-RACKING BUSINESS

The janitor's responsibilities require him to do some work at various hours of the day and night, seven days per week. The necessity of being available to answer emergency calls at any time largely restricts his leisure-time activities to the immediate vicinity of his buildings. He feels the need to get away from the job more often, to get what he calls a "change of scenery." The routine of work becomes monotonous and tiresome, since it constitutes almost his entire life. His spatial restrictions inevitably narrow his interests to neighborhood events, especially those concerning his tenants. He often gossips with and about these people. But even that becomes tiresome in time, and the janitor must find ways to escape the confines of his work area.

He escapes in two ways. In one, he arranges to have a neighboring janitor tend his fires and otherwise assume his duties while he goes out for an evening. Usually, however, he uses a more covert means of "getting away," such as that which Janitor 4 described:

Jeez, this is the worst job a guy could possibly get. That's why I go to the drugstore every day for coffee. It's just to get away from the building and shoot the bull with some different people. It's bad when you have the same damn people to deal with every day.

They know your every move. But you can't shut yourself off from them, because something serious might happen just when you do. It's a nerve-racking business.

A visit to the drugstore, restaurant, or tavern once or twice during the day enables the janitor to "get away" without actually going more than a few minutes' distance from his buildings. While in one of these places he is part of a system of status and roles that separates him from the confines and constraints of his work world.

"Getting away" must be understood in relation to the deep sense of responsibility for the safety of the tenants and buildings that all janitors have. Despite this strong feeling of personal responsibility, janitors cannot indefinitely endure the monotony of routine in an unchanging setting. A thorough "change of scenery" becomes a periodic necessity. However, as Janitor 33 aptly stated, this change is not achieved without qualms:

You still take the chance of getting away even though you leave dangerous equipment behind that's a big responsibility. You're always in tension when you go out. The responsibility is on your mind, but you have to go out once in a while anyway. If something happened it would lay on your conscience the rest of your life.

Janitors are acutely aware of the possibility of a boiler explosion or fire. Their references to "something serious" or "dangerous equipment" are ways of alluding to possible catastrophes that they do not openly discuss. Only a few janitors ever used the word "fire" in its destructive sense when relating their experiences. When they did use the word, it was only to tell about a minor fire caused by a careless tenant. It was a fire during the course of which they exhibited commendable devotion to duty as guardian of the building and its occupants. Janitor 33 recalled an incident of this kind:

The day before Christmas I came home at eleven and picked up the papers from the back stairs as I do about four times a day because they're a fire hazard. At twelve-fifteen a fellow came to my door. "There's a fire upstairs!" I ran out there, and there was smoke all over the place. A guy had left a cigarette on a studio couch. The fire marshal showed me the butt. Only the butt and skeleton of the couch were left. Before the firemen came I protected the rest of the tenants with a fire extinguisher. I pumped water all around that apartment so the fire couldn't get outside.

The dangerous equipment (firebox and boiler) is located in the boiler room of every building. It is dangerous in several ways. Sometimes, for example, gases from garbage accumulate in the firebox so fast that they blow off the furnace doors. This is a personal danger to the janitor, for he spends considerable time in the boiler room every day.

Another danger is that of "flooding" the building. Steam for the heating system is generated in the boiler. A certain amount of water is lost each day in the form of vapor that escapes through the air vent of every radiator. This water is replaced daily by turning on a valve that allows water to flow into the boiler. If, as sometimes happens, the janitor forgets to turn off the valve, incoming water forces its way through the steam lines and finds exits through the air vents. The mental picture of water gushing out of every radiator in the building plagues more than a few janitors. This dangerous possibility is another feature of the work situation that contributes to the janitor's feeling of responsibility. Moreover, it is a threat to his security in the job, since a "flood" is apparently the result of his carelessness. Janitors who have had more than one experience with "floods" are apt to become extremely careful about shutting off the valve controlling the flow of water into the boiler. Janitor 35, who exhibited rather compulsive behavior toward this valve, is an example of how "floods" can affect the janitor's emotional state:

There's one thing that gets me the most and makes me more or less nervous. It practically made a nervous wreck out of me. It happened to me a couple of times that I "flooded" a building. One time it was bad. I'll go back now and check the valve two or three times. I'll get near the door on my way out; and even if I checked the valve before, I still ain't sure, and go back and check it again. The time it was bad made me so blamed nervous. I was so touchy on it you couldn't talk about it to me. It made a nervous wreck out of me. I'll turn on that water valve, turn it off again, check it and check it. And you know, last Sunday I went to church and I wasn't myself there. Even though that morning I went back to check the valve again and again, it played on my mind. It's that way all the time. When I "flooded" here a little bit, it put my nerves on edge again.

Clearly, then, the great responsibility janitors feel can be explained in terms of the janitor's conception of himself as the guardian of the building and its occupants. Being the custodian of the building, and the only representative of the owner on the job, the janitor is largely free to set up his own work schedules and adhere to them as he sees fit. He likes to think that he is his own boss, since his work is seldom supervised. This "own boss" conception fits in very well with the janitor's overprotective attitude toward his buildings and tenants. A brief sketch of the history of the occupation will highlight the significance of these conceptions.

Until a generation ago, almost every janitor was foreign-born. These men had been janitors before their union was organized. Some few were reputedly depraved, and could not hold a job very long. Such men were often exploited by unscrupulous building owners, who forced them to work long hours for small wages, until they drifted off to find work in other buildings. Most janitors, however, were worked too hard for too little to afford the luxury of depravity. Being foreign-born, and somewhat strange and suspicious, they were easily associated with their reputedly debauched fellows by the public at large. Janitors were ascribed a very low occupational status, and an equally low social status. Since the formation of their union, more than fifty years ago, they have gained better and better working conditions and a progressively higher rate of pay. A great many foreign-born janitors have been replaced by American-born janitors who, in many cases, are their sons. Along with these changes, there have developed corresponding changes in the janitor's self-conceptions. I mentioned his efforts to think of himself, and to be thought of generally, as a good mechanic. I have emphasized that he sees himself as a deeply responsible person. He has had less and less supervision, so that today he is virtually independent of direct supervision. All these trends are oriented toward higher occupational and social status. Thus, "own boss," "responsible guardian," and "good mechanic" are self-conceptions that function to disown the janitor's occupational (and corresponding social) heritage, to justify his substantial income[1] (which is close to that of building tradesmen), and to establish his claim to middle-class status.

Although quite independent of direct supervision, the janitor does have occasional contact with his superiors. They are either the owners of buildings in which he works or real-estate agents appointed by them to manage the buildings. The union business agents can tell janitors what not to do, but they are called upon to do this only in very special cases. The janitor's boss, owner or real-estate agent, is ordinarily the only one to whom he must account for the level of his work performance.

The owner may inspect his building as often as he likes, of course, but he actually has little need to inspect if he has confidence in his janitor. Because there is no point in keeping an untrustworthy janitor, the janitor who is kept is likely to be satisfactory in the performance of his routine duties. Hence, the owner seldom has occasion to be on the job.

The union business agent can issue direct orders to the janitor only when he finds that the janitor has violated union regulations. If the janitor does his work properly, he has little contact with the business agent.

The janitor actually is his own boss when he conducts his work activities in a manner that avoids interference. Interference may appear in the form of direct orders from boss and business agent, or in the form of service demands from tenants. In any case, those who interfere contribute toward making janitoring a "nerve-racking business."

MEETING THE PUBLIC

When a janitor says that his is a "nerve-racking job," he is really expressing concern about relationships with tenants. He considers them the primary source of the endless minor annoyances that interfere with his daily routine. One janitor aptly stated this viewpoint:

The first year as a janitor you are sensitive about a lot of things; then you get hardened to it. You get mad at the tenant if she complains, and if the complaint is legitimate you get mad at yourself. Whenever you got to meet the public you kinda gotta put a shell on you, you know. It's like when you have a position of trust. You're blamed if something is found missing, but you never get credit if extras are found.

As in other occupations in which the members' relationships with the public form a substantial part of their work, members of the janitorial occupation are forced constantly to adjust and, in many instances, to cater to the wishes of those they serve. More particularly, the janitorial occupation is one on which the public has, or thinks it has, a claim.[2] In the course of his work, the janitor comes into direct and daily contact with the tenant-public. The tenants, feeling that their individual demands must be catered to at once, often fail to take into consideration the occupational routine and personal life of the janitor. Commenting on this situation, the same janitor quoted above bitterly remarked:

Any time you meet the public and have "fifty bosses," you got it tough. A lot of them think you are a personal servant instead of working for an owner. He expects you to cut down on expenses. The tenants take a different attitude.

The sarcastic reference to "fifty bosses," whose interests are directly opposed to those of his employer, indicates the difficulty with which the janitor is faced when he serves the tenant-public. Because this public is made up almost entirely of housewives, the janitor meets with some peculiar problems.

Housewives spend much of the day in and around their apartments. The janitor also spends much of the day in and around the building. Tenants know when he makes his rounds, as his work is routinized. They are apt to interrupt his work routine at almost any time. Far worse than this, they are inclined to watch for him when he enters his basement apartment to rest. A janitor related how this happens:

The tenants never leave you alone. They know your every move and keep pestering you. When I come in and rest, I like to lay on the rug because it's easier to relax on a hard surface. You know, the tenants can see right in the front window, and they know when I lay down on the rug. But they won't let me rest here. There's always some silly old cow who sees me. When I get settled on the rug, more likely than not some old dame will ring the bell just to ask me how my wife is. And she thinks I should appreciate her concern for my wife, too, after she gets me up like that.

Unless the janitor has his blinds drawn, tenants can see him in his basement apartment. He does not mind if they take advantage of his visibility to tell him about something that he classifies as "serious," but he resents their intrusion upon his privacy for any lesser reason.

The tenants observe the janitor as he performs the activities in his daily routine. As housewives, they are prone to inspect his cleaning activities with considerable care. As tenants, they are likely to expect a high caliber of performance from him at all times. They do not consider that he, like they, may feel ill occasionally and let some of his cleaning work go for another day. This point was made by another janitor:

They can always watch your work. When you don't feel good and let your work go, the tenants begin to kick. If you got a good record, the real-estate office takes your side and explains to them why you haven't been able to do everything. A lot of real-estate agents who stay away from the job will believe that shit; that's why you've got to be careful with tenants. They can make trouble for you, so you have to be careful besides telling them off. Still, there are times when you're not too careful. They can make a helluva lot more trouble for you than you can for them.

Tenants can cause trouble for the janitor by complaining to his superiors about the service. Complaints to the superiors are signs of unsatisfactory service, as well as unsatisfactory relationships between janitor and tenants. Perhaps the lowest blow struck by such complaints is their violation of the janitor's "own boss" conception. Of course, he expects an occasional complaint from his "'fifty bosses," as he has ideas of his own regarding when and how his work should be done. But he particularly dislikes tenants going "over his head" with their complaints. He, the janitor, is in charge of the building. If there is something that displeases the tenants, they should tell him about it, not his superiors.

Even when tenants go directly to the janitor with their complaints, they still interrupt his routine. Moreover, they frequently approach him with what are to them "emergencies," but with what he considers to be nuisances. Such occurrences are all in a day's work when dealing with the public. One janitor replied, when asked about the toughest part of the job:

The toughest part of the job is dealing with the public. Most of the tenants are hard to satisfy. I'd say that about 50 per cent of the tenants you run up against are always nagging you. They want something all the time. They start with that nagging early in the morning, and by the time you are through at night you are all in.

SOME CHARACTERISTICS OF TENANTS

The janitor tends to think categorically about tenants: they are either "good" or "bad." That is, he finds his relationships with them either satisfactory or unsatisfactory. He interacts with them too frequently and too intimately to have neutral feelings about them. His actual depictions of "good" and "bad" tenants closely approximate ideal types. I have done no more than arrange his depictions according to the logical extremes, "good" and "bad" tenants. He was already thinking in terms of such extremes before I met him.

All tenants disturb the janitor's home life part of the time; some, much of the time. He feels that he cannot completely shut himself off from the latter, because he fears something really serious might happen were he to make himself unavailable to them. Those who unnecessarily disturb him at home or interrupt his work routine exhibit one of the traits of "bad" tenants. They are inconsiderate.

Such tenants are inconsiderate in other ways, too. They irk the janitor when they demand immediate service, or demand more service than his job requires him to provide, or, for that matter, when they demand anything. Tenants, he maintains, should *ask* him to perform services that are in his domain. Demands disrupt his work routine and threaten his "own boss" conception. When speaking of tenants who behave in this manner, one janitor said:

A lot are unreasonable in their demands for service. They expect you to drop everything if they have something and take care of them right away. They complain about the heat. Some get up early and want heat early. Some stay up late and want heat late. Some of them want too much service, things that aren't part of my work, that I can't possibly do.

This informant believes that, although he works long hours now, demanding tenants would have him work still longer hours.

When a janitor enters a tenant's apartment to make a repair, she may suddenly find several other things in need of immediate repair. Once tenants "trap" a janitor in their apartment, they expect him to stay until he has every mechanical item in good working order. He resents being lured into their apartments this way, particularly when he has a heavy schedule of work planned for that day. He may have promised other tenants that he would do repair jobs for them that day, but these "bad" tenants do not consider that.

Tenants who habitually tell the janitor all their household troubles are not necessarily demanding, but among them are unthinking usurpers of the janitor's time. The latter feel compelled to stop their janitor whenever and wherever they see him, and blithely reveal their discovery of something else for him to do in their apartment. The following is another janitor's colorful description of such ill-considered behavior:

Man, there are *so* many definitions of a bad tenant. There are what I call pests. Every week they got something for you to do, even if it's just a screw or a bracket. Every time they see you they stop you, even if you're all dressed up, going to the show in the evening. Sure, a few times somebody stopped me at nine or ten o'clock at night when I was dressed up on the way to the show. I tell them to wait with that stuff. I tell them I'm working from five o'clock to at least nine o'clock as it is, and when I get dressed and go out I ain't working and I don't even want to hear about work. Why, I was on vacation once about four hundred and fifty miles from here and some tenant sees me there and tells me that something needs fixing. I just laughed in her face and told her to see me when I got back on the job and not before.

Besides being inconsiderate of the janitor in their demands on his time and effort, "bad" tenants are strikingly uncooperative. The janitor attempts to enlist the tenants' cooperation in complying with the rules of the building, but some of them persistently fail to do so. Such tenants, the janitor asserts, do nothing to keep the building and grounds from becoming dirty and defaced. The following clearly shows the janitor's contempt for them:

It burns you up when people don't try to keep clean, and mess up the place. I just bawled a woman out before. She pushed her baby buggy against the door to open it, and I told her that she should know better than that. It makes all kinds of marks and scratches, just like a garage door, I told her. So the woman gets insulted and says it isn't the first time she ever opened a door. And I said it's a helluva way to do it, though. Kids dirtying the hall and all over—those are the things that aggravate you.

As the above informant bitterly stated, uncooperative tenants are apt to become indignant or defiant when the janitor points out their carelessness to them.

The children of uncooperative tenants, janitors believe, do not receive proper training. Parental instruction to inhibit their destructive behavior seems to be either inadequate or totally lacking. One janitor sarcastically described an incident illustrative of this point:

We "love" tenants when we have a nice lawn in the summer and a woman comes out with two or three kids who have rakes and shovels and she says, "No, children, don't dig." That's really cute.

Another, more flagrant, disregard of the rules of the building is exhibited by tenants who break the rules governing use of the laundry. The schedule of washday allotments is printed on every tenant's lease, or on a placard located on the wall of the laundry, or on both. Much to the janitor's chagrin, some tenants take it upon themselves to wash whenever they are so inclined, thereby disrupting the laundry schedule. Commenting on this, another janitor said:

Some tenants think that because they pay their rent every month they should have more privileges than other tenants. Then when they can't use, say, the laundry room when they want to, even though the schedule is plainly written on the poster in the laundry room, they get mad and say that janitors are dictators telling them what to do all the time. What the hell, you've got to have rules about the use of the building's facilities or else tenants would be scratching each other's eyes out.

The third characteristic of "bad" tenants is their disinclination to appreciate the janitor's efforts to accommodate their whims. One way in which tenants display this characteristic is revealed indignantly by the following janitorial comment:

Janitor burns up if he does right thing and tenants say he didn't. Tenant may tell boss that she tells Joe three or four times to do something and he didn't do it—when she never said a word to me. That makes a fool of you if it ain't so. Tenants like this don't know any better, but what can you do? You can't cook them over, so you get along best you can with them.

What this janitor was getting at is that "bad" tenants do not appreciate his readiness and willingness to help them.

Instead, they put him in a bad light by falsely accusing him of shirking his duties. They do not realize that if they approach him straightforwardly he will do much more for them.

The above informant also alluded to the fourth characteristic of "bad" tenants. They refuse to recognize the janitor as the owner's representative—and a very responsible one, at that. They choose instead to make their complaints or requests directly to the owner or real-estate functionary. In other words, they continually "go over the janitor's head." The janitor finds that such people are usually very cordial in his presence but that their friendly façade is treacherous. One janitor described them in strong terms:

Some of them are so sneaky. They smile at you and ask about the family, and when your back is turned they call the office and complain about you. If a tenant has got something to say, she should say it to me, and we can settle the thing. The ones that argue with me are actually the ones that will back me up when the real-estate agent asks about me. The sweet, smiley ones are the sneaky bastards. When they call the office, the office yells at me, and I yell at the tenants, and nothing gets done.

Janitors contend that the tenants who display the characteristics of "badness" do so not only toward them but toward everyone. To substantiate this contention, the janitor cites considerable supporting evidence of their "'badness." Thus, he points out that they do not teach their children to respect the landlord's property and that they break the rules of the building.

As further evidence of "badness," the janitor reveals that these tenants are lazy. It is his considered judgment that their housekeeping is substandard. He has an opportunity to compare their apartments with the others because he goes through every apartment at least twice a year, when he installs and removes screens. Therefore, for the janitor to maintain that "bad" tenants "are just sloppy—dirty in the house and dirty all over," is to report his observations.

Janitors give many examples to show the different ways in which "bad" tenants are lazy. For instance, another janitor indignantly commented:

This tenant had a stuffed toilet, and I couldn't get up there right away when she called about it. So she said, "What the hell does he do with his time?" What the hell does *she* do, the lazy pup! She's too lazy to take her clothes down. The next one who washes has to do it for her to clear the clotheslines.

Along with the above supporting evidence of "badness," the janitor maintains that "bad" tenants engage in disputes with everyone. As one janitor observed, "I always notice that people like that will fight with everybody: janitor, neighbors, laundryman—everybody."

Such tenants try to misrepresent themselves to others, too. That is, they are "connivers" and "schemers." A janitor and his wife "exposed" one of these people to me:

JANITOR: Not long ago a tenant wanted to take out some insurance on her kid's bicycle. The insurance guy came to me and asked me if she keeps it locked up in the storeroom—I think she really kept it in the laundry room. Anyhow, a year or so later this woman reports her kid's bike stolen. She raised a big stink with the real-estate office about it—told them she didn't have any insurance on it and wanted the laundry room kept locked up.

WIFE: We know darned well that she had insurance on that bicycle, but I'll bet she just wanted to get a new bike. That bike she said was stolen was a sidewalk bicycle, and she must have wanted to get a bigger bike for her kid. I'll bet she planned it that way.

JANITOR: Yeah, I know she musta got insurance on that bike, and she made a big stink about it being stolen so she could get another bike out of the insurance company. Boy, what a cheap trick! But that's what I have to put up with.

"Good" is the polar opposite of "bad." From the janitor's standpoint as well, "good" tenants are the opposite of "bad." If all of his tenants were "good," he would have none of the problems presented in this section. Since it is "impossible to keep all of the tenants happy," some of them will be displeased with the janitor no matter how hard he tries to please them. He is generally successful in establishing amicable relationships with most of his tenants. The relatively few "bad" tenants really cause him an amount of trouble that is far out of proportion to their numbers.

TRAINING TENANTS

The janitor is by no means the passive recipient of his tenants' abuses. Rather, he is very active in trying to change the "bad" tenants into "good," and in trying to keep the "good" ones "good." He believes that by persistently applying the Golden Rule in his relationships with tenants it is inevitable that they will respond favorably. He holds that "if you treat them all right, they treat you all right." The various means by which he "trains" tenants are forms of preparation for application of the Golden Rule.

It is important to point out here that I am presenting only the janitor's views. Very likely, the establishment of good relationships between him and his tenants means a great deal more to him than it does to them. In any disagreement or dispute involving janitor and tenant, the outcome is of much greater significance to him than it is to the tenant. The more control he has over the actions of his tenants, where he is concerned, the more successful a janitor he is. Housewives, in their roles as tenants, do not need to be concerned with self-feelings to the extent that the janitor does. His conceptions of himself are thoroughly wrapped up in his work. He is aware that society judges him, and that he judges himself, largely by the work he does. He is consciously try-

ing to achieve higher status for himself through public recognition of higher work status. His self-conceptions and his
interactions with tenants are oriented toward higher status.
Recall that he is his "own boss," a responsible guardian of
the building and its occupants, and so forth. His relationships with tenants, he believes, must be satisfactory if he is
to be properly recognized. They must be satisfactory to be
consistent with his self-conceptions. Thus, when a tenant-
housewife makes a concession, or "becomes trained," whatever meaning that has for her is minute compared to its
great significance to the janitor.

The ability to "train" tenants is developed over a number of years. It takes time to learn how to deal with the
public. As one janitor said:

It takes a little bit of experience with people. Take a man who
did labor work before, and not janitor work. He will have
trouble. It takes years of experience to learn to deal with people.
If they are right, then you go along with them—it's okay. If you
are right, you stick up for your rights. See, they don't like to be
told by the janitor. If a maid messes up the garbage, you tell the
tenant to tell the maid to clean it up. It's your right to do that.
Some nasty ones tell you to clean it up. They say it's your duty to
do it, and you have to show them they are wrong. You have to
know them. I find out which tenants I can joke with. Others I
say hello to—that's all. Of course, some janitors can be mean when
they don't like a tenant. They can dirty up the bathroom when
they are there, and so forth, but I really blame the tenant then.
If the tenant would treat him nice, he wouldn't do it.

As is pointed out here, "training" tenants involves knowing them quite well and making use of their individual
differences, being firm in correcting their errors, and applying the Golden Rule.

When a tenant is unreasonable in her demands, the janitor ordinarily employs some kind of stalling tactic. This
forces her to wait much longer for his service than she would

have waited had she approached him properly. In an extreme case he may flatly refuse to help her out unless she *asks* him respectfully to make the repair when he can. An eloquent description of this latter procedure was given as follows:

Nothing burns a janitor up more than when a tenant is very demanding. If they tell you they want something done like they was giving you a direct order, then they don't get nothing but shit from me. It's really for the birds when they demand you to do something—and it's always in a hurry, too. They come crying that it's practically a matter of life or death. Maybe they say their apartment is being flooded and when you get there a fuckin' faucet is dripping a little. Boy, does that burn my fuckin' ass! I had a case like that a couple years ago. Some woman comes to me all excited. She says the apartment is full of water. So I go over, and what is it? It's a goddamn faucet leaking slow. So I bawled the hell out of her, and told her that I wouldn't fix that fuckin' faucet for love or money. What the hell does she think I am, I said, dragging me up there in a big fuckin' hurry because she's got a goddamn drip in her faucet. For months she tried to get me to fix it, and I wouldn't have no part of it. She called the real-estate office, and they called me in about it. I told them that even if it meant losing the building I wouldn't fix that faucet. You know what they had to do finally? They had to get a plumber to fix it—I wouldn't do it. Since then, that woman ain't never told me to hurry and do nothing. She always says, "Please come when you have time," and now I take care of her. This demanding-in-a-hurry shit don't go with me. Those fuckin' fourflushers got to ask in a nice way or they don't get me to do nothing.

The above informant was not perturbed by the false alarm itself; rather, he was irked by the circumstances in which the alarm was sounded. The tenant demanded that he come at once instead of asking that he come at his convenience. His stubborn refusal to fix the tenant's faucet, even in the face of being fired, shows how far a janitor may carry his sanctions to force a tenant to make the concessions he desires.

The janitor endeavors to convince tenants that it is both unwise and costly to be careless in ways that create extra work for him. One way of doing this is by threatening to make the careless tenants pay for the services of a building tradesman if they continue creating unnecessary janitorial work.

Some janitors make a point of subtly instructing their tenants to tip them after doing any kind of repair job for them. One janitor proudly explained how he does this:

About this repair business, you know, I always accept cash when I get through with a job—I don't drink. Some tenants offer a drink, but I always refuse. Pretty soon they get it into their heads that I'm a janitor that don't drink, and they offer me a buck when I finish a job. Now, that's okay—that's business. Besides, if you take a drink from them they are always the first to complain that you are always drunk.

The janitor quoted above "trains" tenants to tip him for services rendered *and* to appreciate his efforts to serve them. He considers tips to be a symbol of respect: he receives tips, not drinks, for his special services. He also avoids being associated with the stereotype of the janitor who will do anything for a drink. He wants his tenants to think of him as a sober mechanic, in the business of performing services for them.

The janitor attempts to teach tenants that he is not to be disturbed outside "business hours." To do this, he finds countless ways of demonstrating that unwarranted and ill-considered interruptions of his home life are unfair, immoral, and downright hostile acts. He believes that once he earns the respect of the tenants, they will no longer ring his bell at all hours when they blow a fuse or forget their key. As one janitor stated it:

They disturb me in the daytime, sometimes. Nobody calls at night, like you hear some say. That must be out of respect for me.

I had cases of people breaking in through their kitchen windows, not to bother me at night.

Another example of "training" concerns receipt of tenants' packages. Either the janitor or his wife is almost always at home during the day. As a personal favor they usually receive packages that are delivered when tenants are not at home. But if the janitor is having trouble with a tenant, he can refuse to accept her packages. This constitutes an additional sanction:

If I see they're a nuisance and looking for trouble, I pay no attention to them and pretend they don't even live here. And it hurts them more than it does me. I don't accept packages for them.

I have shown that when a janitor has tenants who respond to the golden rule in undesirable ways, he tries to "train" them. "Training" entails the application of sanctions, ranging from those that are subtly instructive to those that openly threaten. Still, at times nothing seems to work. There are always a few tenants who are apparently "untrainable." They cannot or will not be taught right and proper behavior. Some janitors discover the futility of their "training" efforts in such cases only after experiencing countless frustrations.

My trouble is that I keep arguing with them, and aggravating myself instead of doing something about it. I've thought about doing something about it. I've thought of doing something to them enough.

This janitor has been struggling to reconcile his beliefs with reality. Tenants, he believes, should be able to behave properly, but some of them continue to "aggravate" him. He has even thought of "doing something to them," but what else can he do?

The simplest means employed by janitors to explain the

"untrainables" is to classify them as "nutty" or "nervous" or "just plain ignorant." If a tenant does not respond properly to the Golden Rule treatment, or to "training" for the Golden Rule, there must be something wrong with her. Nothing pleases her. To the janitor's way of thinking, such a tenant is a chronic troublemaker and a chronic complainer. She is "a nutty tenant." He concludes that it is absolutely impossible to establish a good relationship with her. He classifies other "untrainables" as "nervous." He tries to understand and tolerate these tenants:

Boy, when you have a tenant that's a nervous tenant, they're another bad tenant. When you come down to it a man has to use a lot of psychology on this job. You know when a person is mentally ill, and you try to pass it off the best way you can.

Janitors generally believe that they know how to deal with people, as such dealings are of central importance in their job. Janitors who are most successful in relationships with tenants may, as did the above janitor, extend this general belief to the point where they see themselves as psychologists. Thus, when a tenant is "bad" because of what they decide is mental illness, these janitor-psychologists realize that she cannot be "trained," so they accommodate her.

The last group of "untrainables," the "ignorant" tenants, includes all who, according to the janitor, were not reared properly. They, therefore, "don't know what it's all about," because they have never been able adequately to understand the consequences of their acts:

But it goes in the family, the way you are raised at home—that's the way you act. The daughter acts just as filthy as the mother. It's no use making yourself extra trouble hollering at them. You just can't teach them.

Since the janitor is convinced that he cannot "train" these tenants, he devises other methods of minimizing the trouble they can cause him. He does this largely by adopting certain preventive measures, such as those revealed by the following janitor, whom I interviewed while he was mopping vestibules:

How do you like the way it smells in here? It smells like it's been mopped, doesn't it? Well, when they come in and smell it, they know I been here. I used to scrub the vestibule on my hands and knees with kitchen cleanser. I finally found out from an "old-timer" that if you put enough disinfectant in the water and use a mop, they can smell it for three or four days. Before, I used to scrub the vestibules with kitchen cleanser, and if they got dirty a day or two later, I'd get complaints about them. Now I use a mop with this water that has a lot of disinfectant in it, and I don't work nearly as hard or get them nearly as clean, but I never get any complaints, even if they get dirty. As long as they can smell that I been here, they're satisfied. It's all in the mind, I'm telling you. You can fool tenants with steam the same way. Some old woman wanted me to give steam one day when the temperature was in the seventies. I told her to listen for it in a few minutes and went down and tapped on the steam pipe to make it sound like she was getting steam. Next day when I saw her I asked her if she got enough steam yesterday, and she said that it was enough, thank you. See, so long as she thought she heard steam, she felt warm enough. Man, what you have to go through sometimes to keep them happy!

Many complaints are complaints of the senses. Thus, the vestibule has to smell of disinfectant, or else it is not clean; if there is no tapping sound in the radiators, they are not warm enough. The janitor avoids making major concessions through the use of these and similar devices.

Although the janitor attempts to treat all his tenants in conformity with the Golden Rule, he usually tires of working with special diligence to accommodate "bad" tenants. Some janitors "pretend they don't live" in the building. More often, janitors follow the practice of a janitor who said, "The bad ones get treated bad and the good ones get treated good." That is, some of the sanctions used in "training" become somewhat vestigial. They remain in similar forms, but they are no longer crucially important, because the decisive stage in the life cycle of the "bad" tenant is past. Once they are deemed "untrainable," the janitor accommodates them. He may on occasion find their subsequent behavior disquieting. However, such "bad" tenants no longer constitute a dangerous threat to his self-conceptions, despite the limitations they have given to his chances for success in "dealing with the public."

JANITORIAL COLLEAGUE RELATIONSHIPS

Although the janitor works alone, meets and resolves problems in "dealing with the public" in substantial isolation from bosses, union officials, and fellow janitors, he does have occasion to interact with and develop firm judgments about significant others who are not tenants. This section discusses the janitor's work relationships with nontenant, significant others, centering attention on those with whom the janitor has most regular, frequent and, in some respects, most meaningful contact: his janitorial fellows.

Janitors are keenly aware of their occupation's lowly reputation in the community. Yet, as individuals, they develop self-conceptions of the sort that ordinarily would be found in members of established middle-class occupations. How, then, does the janitor reconcile his self-conceptions with corresponding social conceptions of janitors? He uses a simple, clear-cut device. After comparing himself with occupational associates, he tends to agree that the community is right in its evaluation of *them,* but finds that *he* is "different." He agrees that other janitors are unprincipled, disorderly, and irresponsible. However, he, the individual janitor, belongs to the category of practitioners who are morally sound, capable, and responsible. He is the sort of professional person that other janitors *should* be. The following observations illustrate the point:

You know, nine out of ten janitors are no good. They were nothing in the old country. They didn't know nothing there, were pigs or something low class, had no profession, no schooling, and drink most of the time. But that ain't right. Janitor must know plumbing, electricity, about steam and boiler. Janitor should be able to think fast in emergency. Janitor must be trained. In this building, one hundred and fourteen people would suffer if something went wrong.

Besides being unqualified when they enter the occupation, most janitors, according to the individual janitor, are incapable of adjusting to the rigorous personal demands of the work. The work situation causes many janitors to become extremely nervous:

Most janitors aren't as patient as I am, are they? It's all in the head. I've been peaceful for the last twenty years. I used to be jumpy like other janitors, who can't sit still for more than ten minutes.

In various other ways, the individual janitor justifies his belief that he is different from, and better than, other janitors. For example, he indicates that some react to work problems by turning to drink; others support the community's stereotype of janitors by failing to become attentive to details of personal cleanliness and neatness; and still others may even turn to crime, which newspapers eagerly publicize. Thus, the janitor finds scapegoats among his nominal colleagues who, he claims, are *the* degrading elements in the occupation.

Although janitors are, as one of them put it, their "own worst enemy," because they look down on one another and seldom cooperate with one another in the true spirit of colleagueship, the work situation has made it necessary for them to work together in some ways. Primarily responsible for their working together is the seven-day week. In order to have an occasional full evening off, especially during winter, the janitor must find a neighbor whom he can trust to bank his fires for him and be available in case of an emergency. It is for him, together with his colleagues, to work out some system whereby each in turn can spend an occasional evening away from the job. Building-switching is the usual arrangement that they work out.

Building-switching is an informal agreement between two neighboring janitors to take care of each other's fires and be on hand for emergencies when one or the other is out for the evening: "There's another janitor down the street that banks my fires for me and I bank his fires when he goes out. It's a friendly deal—no cash involved." Another said: "'One thing you have to do is work hand-in-hand with another janitor so you can switch off with him. I switch with the fellow next door, and we can get away for a while occasionally."

Building-switching may become so established that janitors who are partners in the arrangement sometimes "cover" for each other routinely in cases of potentially dangerous oversights, as well as obvious emergencies. However, building-switching is not without its weak points. Note what happened to this janitor:

I was switching buildings with a janitor over there, and one day he forgot to fix one of my fires. It was a cold day, too. I got a fifteen-day notice on that building right after that, and that cost me ninety-two dollars a month. And don't think that didn't hurt plenty—right in the ass. He got paid back plenty, alright. Since then he broke his arm and had bleeding ulcers. The Lord pays back those janitors that fuck other people.

Building-switching is an informal arrangement between two janitors to make it possible for each to have an occasional entire evening away from the job. If a partner in this arrangement fails to take care of the other janitor's fires, the other janitor may lose all, or a large part, of his income, for he alone is responsible in such an event. Since, as will be shown later, all janitors agree that "security" is the basic motive for being a janitor, then it is absolutely inexcusable for a janitor to threaten his switching partner's security by "forgetting to fix" his fires. From this perspective, it is quite understandable that the janitor just cited believes that the Lord punishes those janitors who fail their switching obligations.

Generally, switching agreements do run quite smoothly. Whether the parties to such agreements like each other or not is really beside the point. Their need for the agreement is so strong that they are quite satisfied to enter into frankly utilitarian relationships that carry no commitment to explore possibilities for friendships. With respect to this matter, one janitor observed that "friendships between switching partners would be strictly frosting on the cake."

Informal association among janitors is more likely to occur when they meet each other while making work rounds, or when dropping into a neighborhood restaurant or tavern to take a rest break during the afternoon. When asked where janitors meet and what they talk about, one janitor replied:

We talk mostly about the weather, about repair jobs, and sometimes beef to each other about tenants. Some of the janitors I talk to more than others just like other people, because I like some more and others less. When I used to drink more, I got together with some in the liquor store on Marjorie Street in the afternoon. They still hang out there yet. Sometimes I meet janitors in the hardware store over there, and others I meet on the street.

The weather is of great importance to janitors. It often directly affects the amount of work they have to do, and so it is a natural topic of conversation. Talk about repair jobs often involves an exchange of technical information, although the talk may be coated with gripes or braggadocios.

The above casual mention of a liquor store as a local meeting place for janitors is also of interest. Janitors have more free time in the afternoon than in the evening. They retire early because they must arise early. Any drinking that they do, then, is usually done during daylight hours. Liquor stores that have bars seem to cater to men in working clothes. The atmosphere is strikingly informal, and prices at the bar are lower than prices in conventional taverns or cocktail lounges. I spent many afternoons (all in the line of duty!) in a liquor store similar to the one the above janitor mentioned. It will be well to recall some of the observations of janitors that I made in this informal setting.

The observed liquor store is located in a middle-class neighborhood. Taverns in this neighborhood are usually designed to attract the white-collar trade. They do not even have spittoons. The liquor store contains a bar that was obviously designed for spittoon-using, earthier types. It is open to the public, but one seldom sees a woman there. Just as infrequently during daylight hours does one see a man there who is not in working clothes. During daylight hours, the men at the bar are frequently janitors.

These men are neighborhood janitors. At any given time during the day, one can usually find from one to ten janitors there. The atmosphere is often lively with the shouts that accompany an exciting game of shuffleboard, especially when the losing team is obliged to buy the next round of drinks. Most of this activity occurs shortly after noon, when the janitors have finished their morning chores but have not yet begun their afternoon routine. This is the best time of the day to take inventory of the janitors in the liquor store.

The janitors there are both young and old, American-born and foreign-born. They are of several nationality groups, including Austrian, German, Belgian, Lithuanian, and Italian origins. There are both Protestants and Catholics among them. Variations in nationality, age, and religion suggest that the common characteristic that draws them together is their occupation. This suggestion is plausible, but it requires qualification.

I interviewed at various times and places seven janitors who frequent the observed liquor store. With the exception of the two who are brothers-in-law, none of them ever visits any of the others at home. They see each other only on the job or in the liquor store. In this respect the liquor store is like the tavern near an industrial plant, where fellow workers stop in for "one or two with the boys" after work each day. But their reasons for doing so are different. The men from the industrial plant usually work together. Custom requires that they visit the tavern after work. A member of a work group is subject to "kidding" or ridicule if he does not join his fellows there every day. Janitors, to the contrary, work alone. They visit the liquor store during the intervals between the two or three busy periods of the workday. Emergencies may keep one or two of them away on any given day. Bad weather may keep all of them away for a day or two. None of them feels compelled to be there to avoid ridicule. They go to the liquor store to find some relaxation and to tell one another their tenant troubles.

After one of these janitors has had a particularly upsetting experience with a tenant he may go directly to the liquor store, where he is almost sure to find a sympathetic listener, who will readily agree that the tenant is a combination of four-lettered profanities. The janitor's wife, to be sure, is a sympathetic listener and companion, but she, like the tenant, is a woman, and he would rather have male sympathy and companionship once in a while. It is in the liquor store that the janitor finds the sympathetic male companionship that he desires.

In a sense, the liquor store, like the confessional, is a setting for the hearing of sins. The confessional caters to sinners; the liquor store, to those whose dignity has been violated by sinners.

The liquor store is not for janitors a meeting place of work cliques, since janitors go there for personal reasons, and mingle with their fellows on a level somewhere between that of strangers and friendly acquaintances. Their "'friendly stranger" behavior is sociable enough, but not of intimate form.[3] The liquor store functions for them as somewhat of a recreation center, in which catharsis is individually sought.

The almost daily contact which janitors have with one another in the observed liquor store fosters surprisingly little group feeling. To be sure they have much in common and often come to know each other quite well; yet one cannot help but notice their continuing reluctance to discuss any of their work areas besides difficulties with tenants and bad coal. Underlying this reluctance is their fear of each other: they are afraid to trust neighboring janitors with the kind of information that can be used to displace them from their jobs.[4] They get together in the liquor store in spite of their suspicious attitude toward each other. As in building-switching, they *need* each other. In the present case, they use one another as sympathetic listeners to release tensions that arise through interaction with tenants. Relationships in the liquor store, like those in building-switching, are basically utilitarian.

It may be asked, Do janitors ever develop intimate friendships—relationships characterized by intimate form—with their nominal colleagues? The answer is that they do, but only along certain well-defined lines. Kinship is the most universal basis for breaking down barriers that separate janitors. The other oft-used basis is common national origin. Janitors from the same "old country" do occasionally become close friends. In their case, ethnic ties apparently supersede the individualistic tendencies generally found in members of the occupation:

I'd say that janitors clan together if they are the same nationality. American-born janitors hardly neighbor with each other at all. Neighboring among janitors just depends upon the type of janitors in the neighborhood. They come from the same country and that's what draws them together; not because they do the same work—probably in spite of it.

After agreeing that janitors neighbor along nationality lines, if at all, another janitor remarked:

I never been in another janitor's house, except for a beer. It isn't like a gang working and visiting together. We never do it—I don't know why. We're more or less for ourselves.

A class of activities, referred to by janitors as "cut-throating," is largely responsible for the social distance that janitors maintain among themselves. They define cutthroating as any act, or series of acts, through which a janitor underhandedly replaces, or attempts to replace, another janitor in one or more of the other janitor's buildings. There are four commonly used methods which predatory janitors use in overt attempts to "steal" other janitors' buildings. Overt cutthroating consists of acts that are manifestly calculated to produce quick building-stealing results. I shall mention three of them briefly, and illustrate the fourth.

The union's business agents are reputed to be, and doubtless have at times been, party to cutthroating activities. Janitors generally believe that covetous fellows have literally bought better building assignments from certain unscrupulous business agents.

A second overt cutthroating act is that of letting water

run unchecked into the boiler of the desired building. The janitor presently assigned that building would find his apparent negligence most difficult to explain. Janitors spoke of this more than of any other cutthroating method.

A third method of overt cutthroating involves "stool-pigeoning." In countless ways, the janitor's wife assists him in the performance of his duties. Nearly all these ways are violations of union regulations. A janitor who has a predatory neighbor believes he is always in danger of being reported to the union for these and other violations of regulations, any of which can lead to loss of present building assignments.

A fourth overt cutthroating procedure entails approaching another janitor's boss to persuade him that he is now talking to the best man for his building. In bitter tones, one janitor recalled his experience with so-called friends who had used this means of cutthroating:

Listen, I don't have nothing to do with any janitors. There's one thing I've learned the hard way, and it's this: Don't get too friendly with other janitors. If you do, they'll cut your throat first chance they get. See, they find out how much you make and get jealous if you're making more. They try like hell to take your buildings away from you even if you've done all kinds of favors for them. Four guys, four different guys that I got into the union, mind you, turned around and took buildings away from me. There was one of them who wasn't making so good so I gave him one of three six-flats that were owned by the same guy. What do you think he did? He went to the owner and tried to get the other two six-flats from me, the dirty son of a bitch. I'm telling you, you can't trust nobody in this fuckin' racket. You're better off by yourself. Them other guys are all out to cut your throat if you let them. If you stay away from them and they don't know nothing about you, you're better off, I know.

Besides overt cutthroating, predatory janitors may also engage in building-stealing activities which on the surface appear nonpredatory. This more subtle form of cutthroating is probably an outgrowth of overt cutthroating. The fear of manifestly predatory actions leads janitors to become suspicious of their neighbors. Suspicion makes it difficult for neighboring janitors to cooperate in restricting their level of effort on the job. A janitor who has designs on his neighbor's building can take advantage of the situation by consistently keeping his level of effort above that of his neighbor. The following reveals some subtle cutthroating acts:

Now, take me—I'm lucky I'm alone on this block. The only other building I haven't got is that six-flat next door. My mother-in-law owns it, and Joe is janitor there. I don't have to worry about cut-throating, you see. Take the case where a janitor has three big buildings in a row like I have, and say there's a two-flat next to them that another janitor has got. Say it's a snowy day. Well, what that other janitor does is clean away the snow real quick all the time and keep the two-flat building looking spic and span. Pretty soon one of your owners asks you why you don't get the snow shoveled so fast and neat like the janitor who has the two-flat does. Then you tell him that it takes more time for you because you have so much more to do than the other guy. Then the owner says that if that's the case he'd better give his building to that other janitor. Some janitors are pretty smart, and they pull that stuff on each other to get their buildings away from them. Out east of here, where the apartment buildings are thicker than flies, it's really terrible. When one janitor is seen on the street with a mop in his hand, every janitor on the street gets his mop and lets everybody know he's got his mop out, too. When one mops, they all mop. Man that's rough. There are too many janitors over there.

The janitor is extremely conscious of his neighbors' level of effort, lest he be obviously outdone by them. In an industrial plant, fellow workers commonly cooperate to restrict production.[5] Rate-busters there are severely ostracized by their fellow workers for fear of a step-up in the group's expected level of effort. Since janitors do not work together, are individualistic, and are often suspicious of their neighbors, they seldom cooperate to restrict "production." When a neighbor is obviously doing a much better job, he is considered by the next janitor as a serious security threat. The janitor next door is then in danger of losing a large part of his income. There is really no group of fellow workers to apply sanctions to bring the neighbor "into line." He creates a problem the janitor next door must meet by himself. The above description of the mop situation is further evidence that janitors are wary of their neighbors. It is also further evidence that janitors respond to rate-busting individualistically: "When one mops, they all mop."

There certainly must be some way to establish a good defense against the predatory activities of neighboring janitors and the business agent, or most janitors would assuredly be hopelessly insecure in their occupation. Further, they would probably have even less contact with one another than they do now. There would be little building-switching, hence little opportunity to take an occasional entire evening off. There would probably be no opportunity for liquor-store contacts to function as they do to ease the burdens of work life. A clue to the defense janitors find they must adopt is contained in the advice an old janitor (Number 31) gave to a young janitor when the latter had unwittingly revealed the subtle cutthroating activities of his neighbors:

I'll tell you advice that I gave to that young fellow, Joe, that I bowl with. He has had a lot of trouble keeping buildings. I tell him to do extra things for the landlord, and don't listen to neighborhood janitors about doing nothing, because then they steal your buildings.

The old janitor above advised a young janitor to do extra work for his landlord as the best defense against predatory neighbors. But why do more work than necessary? Janitors have a union to define their level of effort so that landlords will be prevented from exploiting them by demanding that they do "extras." Why do more than the union rules call for? Does not the union protect janitors from exploitive landlords? The union does, but who protects janitors from predatory janitors and union business agents? The only ones janitors can turn to are their bosses, the landlords. Their landlords are their only protection against cutthroating, both by other janitors and by the business agents. That is why many janitors are quick to point out that "a janitor should work in the interests of the owner":

Nobody is going to try to take your buildings if you do your work, because they know that it would be foolish to try. There are some young janitors who are pretty independent and don't do any more work than they can get by with. They aren't very smart. They will lose some buildings before they get much older. They should begin to learn that they can't do nothing, and demand extra pay for anything that they do. A janitor should work in the interests of the owner—I mean he should do his work and not look for extra pay. That way he doesn't have to watch for getting his throat cut. A janitor who does his work shouldn't worry about being friends with other janitors, or anybody else.

The ironic situation that the janitor is in with respect to cutthroating was made quite clear by the above janitor. If a janitor establishes a good relationship with his owner(s), presumably by doing a little more than is required of him, his owner will refuse to listen to tempting offers made by other janitors, or even to offers made by the business agent on behalf of other janitors. If the janitor's work pleases his owner, then his business agent cannot replace him. When an owner is unconcerned about what janitor he has, the business agent appoints one for him. Otherwise, the business agent only recommends janitors to owners. A janitor must be caught breaking union rules to be fired by the owner, or to be removed from the job by the business agent. If a janitor does his work properly, the business agent cannot remove him from his job without being in collusion with the owner. If he does his work properly, and establishes a friendly relationship with his owner, the janitor has a perfect defense against any kind of cutthroating. What the janitor's most secure defense amounts to is running to the arms of those against whom janitors are organized—the landlords—to seek protection from those with whom janitors are organized—fellow janitors and union officials. This is the ironic result of cutthroating.

Perhaps I have led the reader to believe that every janitor resents his neighbor who makes more money than he does. This, of course, is not true. Nor is it true that every janitor who makes more money than his neighbor avoids associating with him for fear of being cutthroated. But it is true that the fear of cutthroating, if not the prevalence of cutthroating, is strong and general enough in the occupation to stand in the way of more intimate colleague relationships, which are requisite to group solidarity.

THE JANITOR'S CAREER

Janitors work for security and toward prestige. In this section, I shall analyze the security-prestige motif of the janitor's career by first considering his occupational choice patterns, second his conceptions of success and retirement, and third the contingencies which significantly affect his level of success and his movement toward retirement.

I have neither interviewed nor heard of a janitor who as much as suggested that he had ever aspired to being a janitor. Without exception, all janitors interviewed were either "forced" into the occupation by the necessity of earning a living, or "somebody talked [them] into it." Other reasons to qualify these two general apologies ran as follows: "I needed an apartment," "I like outdoor work," "I didn't like night work," and so on.

There are some noteworthy differences in patterns of job

entry that distinguish foreign-born janitors from American-born janitors. Most foreign-born janitors have a rural-European background. Many of them came to this country as young men, and settled in the city where they were employed as laborers. Others settled in rural areas where they were employed as "hired hands." As a group they were unskilled and uneducated. They had friends or relatives who had immigrated to this country before them and who had helped them to secure better jobs that ultimately led to janitorial careers.

American-born janitors are usually sons or relatives of European-born janitors. Few of them became janitors without trying other work first, and none of the few did so by choice. All either were unemployed or had "not very good jobs" just prior to becoming janitors. This they had in common with European-born janitors. The big difference is that American-born janitors had loftier aspirations, committed as they were to the American dream of success that anybody can be a success if he works hard and gets the breaks. Thus, many American-born janitors became janitors because they failed *not* to become janitors. They were "born into the game," and reluctantly came back to it after trying to develop careers in other lines of work. The son of a European-born janitor said:

I'm originally a family janitor. My dad was a janitor for thirty years. I was born into the game. I was a shipping clerk, a truck driver, worked in a foundry. Nothing really paid. Now I'm in one way my own boss, and I can work when it suits myself.

When men are hungry and they see a janitor friend who is eating pork chops while they are eating neck bones, the apparent security of janitoring strongly appeals to them:

I got into the racket through a friend of mine, an old foreigner, thirteen years ago, during the Depression. In them days he was eating big pork chops when other people were eating neck bones.

I ain't never forgot that. He told me this was the best racket to get in if you like your stomach. I like my stomach, you see.

Men become janitors, and stay on as janitors, to enjoy economic security. The technical or manual aspects of the job are fairly routine and readily mastered. If the work situation presents any significant challenge, it must challenge not his technical but his social skills. And, indeed, so it does. The real challenge in the work situation comes from the tenants. The janitor defines success in terms of his relationships with tenants.

It is well to recall that janitors are extremely self-conscious about their low occupational and social status. They believe that janitoring relieves them of concern over economic security. When an occupational group establishes its economic security, it apparently then becomes concerned with its status. In so doing, it may meet with resistance from a number of quarters, one being those it serves. Janitors certainly meet with such resistance from tenants. Janitors want to be recognized as respectable human beings. They persistently try to teach their tenants to be more respectful, more cooperative, and more considerate of them. Since each janitor has his own set of tenants, it is his individual problem to develop agreeable relationships with them. No matter what his income is in comparison to the incomes of other janitors, the individual janitor thinks of himself as a success only if he has earned the right to say that he has "good" tenants. For this reason success has no necessary association with income. Success to the janitor is a prestige goal, a desire for recognition by the tenant-public as a dignified human being.

The equivalency of "good" tenants to success was pointed out by one janitor as follows:

Look, money ain't everything. If you have to work your ass off to save dough to invest, then I'd call a guy like that a damn fool. He ain't successful; he ain't living. He's just burning himself out, and all he'll have to show for it will be poor health. If you have good tenants, that's what's really important in being a success.

Making the same point, another janitor stated:

If you are ambitious, have common sense, are alert, then you do well. I don't call living like a dog, saving every nickel to buy property being a success.

While it is true that, in the view of janitors, size of income and accumulation of wealth have no necessary association with success, but are commonly thought of in relation to retirement, they nevertheless are sometimes associated with success. This association is explained by the fact that it is rare for a janitor actually to retire, even if he has enough money to do so. Janitors who reputedly have become wealthy are discussed by their colleagues. These exceptional men have become almost legendary. All janitors have "heard of" them, but few know them. So janitors talk about these "successful" men, not always without envy:

The only way to be a success is to take a risk buying property and not eat good to save money to do it with. Not me. If there's one thing I'll do, I'll eat, even if there's nothing left for anything else.

The above comments show how conflicting values in the occupation provide janitors with a ready justification for modest circumstances. On the one hand, janitoring is an occupation for men who want a good steady income. Yet, some of them are known to have sacrificed, saved, and invested in risky real-estate deals, which in fact returned huge profits. They have become almost legendary figures because the other janitors do not conceive of success in such terms. The janitor considers these relatively few men to be both heroes and fools. They have become successful entrepreneurs, but they have had to "live like a dog" in the process.

Such marginal cases, where success and wealth have been associated, lend further support to the janitor's belief in the entrepreneurial aspects of the occupation. It is of interest to see how the janitor more explicitly conceives of his occupation as a means to an end. This end is retirement.

Retirement is the occupational goal. The janitor has an intense wish to retire—the sooner, the better. Attainment of this goal requires accumulation of sufficient funds, either invested or cash. Janitors think of the occupational goal as the termination of distasteful work: "The basic thing we janitors talk about is to acquire property for income, and retire. This isn't the type of job you do for pleasure, like a profession. You have to set a different goal."

This comment reveals an attitude that is dominant in the occupation. The janitor asserted that the nature of the work determines the occupational goal. Probably, the more distasteful the work, the more fanciful the goal.

In reality, janitors rarely reach their retirement goal. There are two principal reasons for this. First, the union restricts the janitor's income. He can serve no more buildings than he can handle himself. Second, it is difficult to save and invest money when there is little or none left at the end of the month, after eating and drinking well, and making payments on the new car and other expensive status symbols. The janitor nevertheless avidly discusses retirement with his colleagues. He looks forward to the day when he will somehow be able to retire.

I have been developing the point that janitors talk and dream about retiring, but rarely does a janitor actually reach this goal. The janitor's concept of success makes "success" so much of a process that his attempts to achieve it as a state of affairs are less than satisfactory. Certainly the burdens of work life, the daily interactions with tenants, are easier to endure if he can look forward to the time when he retires. The function of the retirement goal is to enable him to do just that. For the entire occupation, the retirement goal is a collective representation that helps to support the janitor's faith in the notion that someday he will join the dignified ranks of the retired. The retirement goal is an occupational fiction: it is much more fancy than fact. Having the functional characteristics of a myth,[6] it may well be called an occupational myth.

The janitor's career rests on security, and moves toward success and retirement. Career contingencies that affect this movement are of two kinds, one having to do with success, the other with retirement.

I have been showing that the janitor feels successful when his tenants seem to act cooperatively, considerately, and respectfully toward him. He then calls them "good" tenants. He talks at length about the social skills he develops to "train" them and keep them "trained." What he really means is that these tenants have certain personal attributes and social attitudes that enable him to be more or less successful in "training" them to cooperate with him and respect him for what he thinks he is.

Elsewhere[7] I have shown that it is easiest for a janitor to be a success when he serves buildings that are occupied by "rich" (that is, upper-middle-class and upper-class) tenants. Unless a janitor chances to work in such buildings, he may never realize that success problems are minimal where tenants are predisposed to engage their janitor in mutually acceptable status relationships. He may be working for their "middle" tenant (that is, working-class, or lower-middle-class) neighbors, and never adequately understand why some of his tenants are "troublemakers." He knows that some of his "middle" tenants are particularly easy to work with, but again he does not often know why. The janitor often fails to notice that those whom he thinks of as nuisances are tenants who incomes are marginal to his. For example, one janitor who has "middle" tenants, contended that "middle-aged

people make the best tenants." Another janitor, who also
has "middle" tenants, asserted that "young people between
the age of twenty-five and thirty-five are the best tenants."
These two janitors, and many others in similar situations,
are groping for *the* answer to their tenant-"training" problems but have overlooked their main source of difficulty:
the "fourflushers."

A janitor knows who of his tenants are "fourflushers."
He knows that such tenants pretend to have more wealth
than they actually have. They are people who "live from
hand to mouth," and he knows it. He despises their unwarranted condescending and demanding attitude toward him,
and they resent his obvious economic prowess. Some janitors
are quick to recognize that the "fourflushers" are the worst
tenants. As one janitor observed, "The people that don't
have anything put up the biggest front and squawk a lot."
And another janitor noted that "some are jealous. They
don't like to see you make too much money."

Janitors take an important step toward success when they
understand why some tenants are easier or harder to "train"
than others. Failing this, they very likely will make no effort
to secure employment in a building occupied by "rich"
tenants. If they remain in lower-middle-class surroundings,
they will have to become much like the janitor who succeeded by "dominating the tenants and making them like
it." Evidently, few janitors are as capable as this man in such
circumstances.

Crucial to success in any type of building is the support
of the janitor's boss. The janitor cannot readily "train"
tenants if his boss (owner or real-estate agent) does not give
him almost complete authority to "run the building" as he
sees fit.

The development of certain insights and personality
characteristics is a decisive attribute of a successful janitor.
Some janitors become excessively emotional when interact-

ing with tenants. Some fail to understand them, and some fail to use expedient methods of working with them. Unless janitors learn to make self-demands congenial with role-demands, they are always on the defensive toward tenants.

The foregoing are indicative of the many crucial decisions, crucial insights, and crucial circumstances that determine success. The dynamics of success in janitoring can be understood adequately only after considering such contingencies as these.

Turning now to the contingencies influencing progress toward retirement, it is evident that they all center around the acquisition and accumulation of money. Acquiring money entails working in a lucrative building, or working in several buildings, the total salary from which is above average for janitors. As one janitor remarked, "You have to know somebody to get good buildings—real estate [agent], owner, or business agent." A janitor must establish friendly contacts with these people, any one of whom can place him in better-paying buildings. His success or failure in doing so will in large measure determine his later ability to retire.

Besides getting better buildings through friendly contacts with owners, the janitor can even get an investment loan from a boss with whom he is on "real good terms":

If the landlord and you are on real good terms, and he lends you money for an investment and you get ahead, the next guy [janitor] can't figure it out. He can't figure where you got the money for a big deal. You just keep your mouth shut so you don't spoil a good thing.

A secret investment loan from an owner may help a janitor toward retirement and also cause his fellows to look on him with envious wonder, since they know how difficult it is to save.

Contacts with owners and real-estate men are helpful in another way. These men can give the janitor good investment advice, once he has accumulated capital and expressed a desire to speculate or invest:

Janitors, you know, really know real estate, if anybody does, because they spend their lives at it. They have contacts, and a lot of them acquire real estate when they get enough money together.

Perhaps the contingency most closely related to retirement is the decision the janitor must make relatively early in his career. He must decide between a standard of living oriented toward the present and a standard of living oriented toward the future. If he chooses the former, he will eat exceptionally well and purchase expensive material goods. If he decides on the latter, he will live a considerably more simple life. Earlier discussion of the retirement goal has offered ample evidence to show that most janitors orient their standards of living toward the present.

CONCLUSIONS

I have shown how the big-city apartment-building janitor meets with interferences of various kinds, especially in relationships with tenants but also in relationships with fellow janitors, bosses, and union officials. These people interfere with his work performance, his efforts to establish job security, his movement toward higher status, and related matters. But life is like that in the big city. Urbanites are continually interfering with one another, consciously and unconsciously, altruistically and selfishly, with and without support from the Almighty. They are continually intruding upon mandated areas of activity, of residence, and indeed of thought. They are continually claiming rights and wrongs for themselves and each other, and are continually seeking ways of backing up their claims with voluntary associations, family traditions, occupational codes of behavior, as well as with laws. There is nothing really peculiar or bizarre about the ulcerating interferences that the janitor reports when discussing relationships with tenants. For it is very likely that, in the view of his tenants, he is also interfering with their lives in significant ways. Their problem is one of mandate. They simply have not clearly agreed on their reciprocal rights and obligations; they are in process of defining their status positions, and learning to express them in role relationships with each other.

The human and moral tensions that accompany, and accrue from, claims and counterclaims of mandates are not peculiar to the big city, but they certainly are chronic there. And they pervade all areas of human activity there, where rapid change and experimentation with life styles foster highly tentative, groping attitudes toward ideas, men, acts, and artifacts. My story of the apartment-building janitor illustrates well some of the basic problems of all workers, and also of all residents, in urbanized areas of our society. The problem of the mandate is only one of many that accompany efforts to achieve feelings of adequacy, certainty, and acceptability in an urban setting.[8]

NOTES

1. The janitor is paid on a sliding scale that reflects the rent levels of apartments he serves. In short, the higher the rent, the more he is paid per apartment served. Thus, if he serves a building that has fifty apartments and charges high rent, he is paid more than he would receive if rents were lower there.
2. Others, such as the teaching occupation, meet similar situations. Teachers must function, occupationally and "socially," under the careful scrutiny of the community, and must somehow adjust to its "interferences." I shall return to this point later, when I discuss the general problem of occupational mandate.
3. I refer here to Georg Simmel's observation that content of interaction may be intimate while form of interaction remains nonintimate. Intimate form occurs where interactors commit themselves to their relationship, feeling that their social and self-identities heavily depend on its existence, See K. H. Wolff (ed.), *The Sociology of Georg Simmel* (Glencoe, Ill.: The Free Press, 1950), p. 127.

4. I refer here to a practice known among janitors as stealing buildings. I shall shortly discuss this practice in some detail.
5. I agree with Everett Hughes that this is a value-loaded concept. See Hughes's discussion of it in *Men and Their Work* (Glencoe, Ill.: The Free Press, 1958), pp. 47–48.
6. G. SOREL, *Reflections on Violence,* trans. T. E. Hulme (New York: Peter Smith, 1941), pp. 126–167.
7. This portion of the present discussion is based largely on my essay "Janitors Versus Tenants: A Status-Income Dilemma," *American Journal of Sociology,* LVII, March, 1952, pp. 486–493.
8. This concluding statement would be incomplete without explicitly acknowledging my debt to Professor Everett Hughes, whose influence on my report on janitors should be evident to all students of work. When Hughes, acting as my thesis supervisor, began reading verbatim accounts of my interviews with janitors, he filled the margins of interview transcripts with comparisons of janitors with physicians and other established professionals. He was obviously extremely excited and enthusiastic about my data, for reasons which for the most part escaped me initially. Then his marginal comments began to hit home, and I was able to share at least some of his excitement and enthusiasm. He had discovered an important methodological point in comparing my study, and other studies of low-status occupations which some of his graduate students were then doing, with studies of the professions. Shortly afterward, Hughes published some comments on this point, which he subsequently republished in a book containing a collection of his essays on work. I wish to conclude by quoting from the latter volume a portion of his comments:

"At first, I thought of these studies as merely interesting and informative for what they would tell about people who do these humbler jobs, i.e., as American ethnology. I have now come to the belief that although the problems of people in these lines of work are interesting and important as any other, their deeper value lies in the insights they yield about work behavior in any and all occupations. It is not that it puts one into the position to debunk the others, but simply that processes which are hidden in other occupations come more readily to view in these lowly ones. We may be here dealing with a fundamental matter of method in social science, that of finding the best possible laboratory for study of a given series of mechanisms" (Hughes, *op. cit.,* p. 49).

2

Manning the Machines—
The Assembly-Line Worker

ELY CHINOY

EVER SINCE the moving assembly line emerged, full-blown, in the Ford Motor Company plant in Highland Park, Michigan, in 1913, it has been a dominating symbol of modern industrialism. Its productive capabilities have epitomized the fruitfulness of mass production; "the new Messiah," Henry Ford called it. Its impact upon workers, cruelly portrayed for all the world to see in such classic films as René Clair's *A Nous la Liberté* (1931) and Charles Chaplin's *Modern Times* (1936), have posed in extreme form the human problems created by mechanization.

The assembly line achieved its symbolic importance despite the fact that it has never enlisted the efforts of most workers, even in the automobile industry with which it is usually most closely identified. No more than 18 percent of production workers in the automobile industry have ever been classified as "assemblers" by the Bureau of Labor Statistics in its studies of wages in 1922, 1925, 1928, 1940, 1950, and 1957—and not all assemblers perform their tasks on a moving line. The maximum proportion of assemblers was reached only in the most recent (1957) wage survey, at a time when the computer already seemed to be replacing the assembly line as the symbol of advancing industrialization.

Despite these relatively limited numbers, assembly-line work seemed for a long time to represent the future, the end result toward which the continuing mechanization of production was headed. The principles upon which moving assembly rests are readily applied to many other kinds of industrial operations; a substantial, even if undeterminable, number of other workers—paint sprayers, polishers, welders, upholsterers, for example—have therefore been subject to the same kinds of job experience as those engaged in line assembly. In addition, the presence of the assembly line has significantly affected the prevailing temper of work and of worker-management relations in those industries in which it has been widely adopted: automobiles, rubber, and meat-packing.

Although essentially a product of the twentieth century, the assembly line rests upon old and familiar principles of production: the division of labor, the use of standardized interchangeable parts, and the utilization of a moving conveyor to bring needed materials to the worker in order to minimize his movements. The division of labor, of course, dates back to the dawn of human history. Plato's classic examination of the principle in *The Republic* is a familiar one, as is Adam Smith's discussion in *The Wealth of Nations*. The first significant use of interchangeable parts is attributed to Eli Whitney in his Connecticut gun plant; with improving metallurgical knowledge and skill, standardized parts were increasingly utilized in many other industries during the nineteenth century. Antecedents of the moving conveyor can be found in the inventions of Oliver Evans, an ingenious Yankee mechanic who built a totally automated grain mill in 1784–1785, in the manufacture of ship's biscuits in the British Victualling Office early in the nineteenth century, and here and there in subsequent years in other British industries. A full-fledged continuously moving conveyor appeared around 1870 in meat-packing plants in Cincinnati, facilitating the "disassembly" of hogs and cows. The contribution of Henry Ford and his co-workers, rapidly copied by his competitors, lay in combining these principles into an integrated system of production.

Introduction of the moving assembly line was in large measure merely a continuation and extension of changes already under way in the Ford plant. When a new building was erected in Highland Park in 1910, a drastic rearrangement of machines took place. The conventional practice had placed all machines of the same type in one place—lathes in one department, milling machines in another, and so on. In order to facilitate the movement of materials through the plant, conventions were ignored, and the machines were rearranged in the sequence in which the operations they performed contributed to the finished product. Various mechanical means of moving parts from one machine to another—gravity slides, for example—were then gradually introduced.

Specialization and continuous division of labor were also taking place rapidly in the assembly both of components and of the finished product even before the moving line was introduced. Final assembly, for example, had originally been a highly skilled job. Each car was put together in one spot by a number of all-around mechanics. By 1913 these skilled workers had been replaced by several less skilled men each of whom was responsible for only one part of the total job. Greater speed and efficiency were also achieved by using "stock runners" who brought necessary tools and materials from the tool crib or parts bin, thus freeing the more skilled workers from the necessity of moving away from their tasks. But when one car was completely assembled, the entire crew still had to move along to another station to start again on another car.

Moving assembly was first introduced in the manufacture of magnetos, then of axles and motors. So successful were these innovations that final assembly could not keep pace with the flow of parts until Ford and his engineers and technicians applied the same techniques to the task of putting together the finished product. The first experimental moving final assembly was pulled along the floor by a rope and windlass. When it proved to be successful, more efficient conveyors were built, and the rest of the plant was totally reorganized to take advantage of the new techniques.

From management's point of view, the assembly line possesses many impressive advantages. By bringing parts to the worker, often along a secondary conveyor as well as on the main line, it eliminates almost entirely the time spent by labor in moving, unproductively, from place to place. Continual rationalization of the assembly process makes it possible to carry the division of labor almost as far as it can go; the ideal assembly line, wrote Henry Ford, would limit each worker to doing "as nearly as possible one thing with only one movement." As Adam Smith pointed out long ago, such a simplification of tasks also increases the proficiency and speed with which each worker performs his job. Perhaps more important, however, the moving assembly line provides management with an extremely efficient device for determining the speed at which men must work. Unlike other machine jobs that can be regulated only by imposing production standards that workers must meet in order to hold their jobs or make adequate earnings, assembly-line jobs can be mechanically controlled; the time allowed for each task depends upon how fast the line moves in front of the worker.

Despite this distinctive characteristic, work on the assembly line obviously possesses many of the same features as do other kinds of routine industrial jobs. Like most semiskilled labor, it is highly repetitive, although on the line, as in other routine work, some jobs are, of course, somewhat more varied than others. Ford's ideal of a single motion continuously repeated at high speed is realized in relatively few assignments, and jobs differ in the number of operations they actually require. In a sample of assembly-line workers studied by Charles R. Walker and Robert H. Guest, for example, over 30 percent performed only one operation (which usually required several motions), 35 percent did from two to five operations, 16 percent had jobs requiring six to ten, and another 15 percent more than ten. The differences in repetitiveness—and the nature of the tasks— can be seen in the following descriptions of jobs by several workers:

(1) I work on a small conveyor that goes around in a circle. We call it a "merry-go-round." I make up zigzag springs for front seats. Every couple of feet on the conveyor there is a form for the pieces that make up the seat springs. As that form goes by me, I clip several pieces together, using a clip gun. I then put the pieces back on the form, and it goes on around to where other men clip more pieces together. . . . The only operation I do is work the clip gun. It takes just a couple of seconds to shoot six or eight clips onto the spring, and I do it as I walk a few steps. Then I start right over again.

(2) As the body shell moves along the line, I start putting a baffle windbreaker (two fenders fit on it) by putting in four screws. Then I put nine clips at the bottom which hold the chrome molding strip to the body. On another type of car there is a piece of rubber which fits on the hood latch at the side and keeps the hood from rattling. I drill the holes in the rubber and metal and fit two screws in. Also, I put four clips on the rubber in the rear fender. On another type of body, I put the clips on

the bottom molding, and in the trunk space I put two bolts which hold the spare tire clamp. I repeat these things all the time on the same types of car.

This latter job required about two minutes to complete, in contrast to the few seconds required for the other.[1]

Both machine operators and men assigned to the line require little training. Semiskilled operatives' jobs, by definition, can be learned relatively quickly and easily, although there are inevitably some differences from one task to another. The first job described above, for example, took only two days to learn, according to the worker, plus a few days more "in order to do it like I do it now." The second job, its holder reported, required a month to master. The basic knowledge needed for routine tasks is usually rapidly gained, perhaps in no more than a few hours or even, on the simplest job, in a few minutes. "Learning" consists chiefly in developing a reasonable degree of mechanical proficiency rather than acquiring an understanding of tools and materials, mastery of complex physical skills, or the ability to exercise judgment in making decisions.

Elimination of any substantial degree of skill from routine tasks is made possible by the predetermination of tools and techniques by engineers and technicians. Each operation is precisely defined, tools are placed exactly where they are needed, and the amount of time allowed for a particular task is set, within close limits, by time-and-motion-study specialists. In a European clothing firm studied by Georges Friedmann, for example, assembly-line techniques had been applied to dressmaking, and the operation to be performed on the conveyor belt were broken down into times measured by the one-hundredths of a minute.[2] (Similar methods of analysis are also applied, of course, to other repetitive tasks.) Little is left for the operatives on most routine repetitive tasks except acquisition of "speed, precision, and dexterity," or, as some English investigators have described it, of "speed as a skill."[3]

Although assembly-line jobs thus resemble other routine industrial jobs in their repetitiveness, the absence of skill, and the predetermination of tools and techniques, they often differ in the demands they make on the worker's attention. Many other routine tasks allow the worker to perform his duties almost automatically while daydreaming, pursuing his own serious thoughts, or carrying on an easy conversation with his fellows. Work on the line, in contrast, frequently requires consistent attention without seriously engaging the worker's interests or demanding the close concentration inherent in skilled labor. One worker in a plant studied by the writer described this feature of assembly-line work as follows: "Most of the time you don't get a chance to think of anything. If you take your mind off what you're doing, you don't get the work done right." Significantly, many studies have shown that repetitive jobs which allow free-roaming fantasy or organized thought or easy social relations are less fatiguing than those that, as Walker and Guest have described most assembly-line jobs, "require a high and continuous degree of mental attention without accompanying mental absorption."[4]

The decisive difference between the assembly line and other semiskilled tasks, however, is "mechanical pacing," control by the line of the speed at which men must work. When the speed of the machine or the rate of production is under the worker's control it can be varied in relation to his energies and feelings. Although high production standards or rigorous discipline may force him to work constantly at high speed, he can slow down if he gets tired or can go faster if he feels especially good. He can work at top speed for a while and at a more leisurely tempo at another time. If necessary he can stop the machine completely. None of

these possibilities is usually available to the man on the
assembly line. Even those jobs that do not impose a rigid,
unchanging speed—and there are some such jobs—allow
only a limited amount of variation in rhythm and speed of
work. On some jobs the worker can occasionally manage to
perform his assignment in less than the time allotted to him;
then, if space permits, he can move up the line a few extra
feet and eventually have a few seconds free for a momentary
break in the otherwise constant tempo. "What you try to
do," one worker observed, "is get a job that you can do in
forty-five or fifty seconds when you have sixty seconds in
which to do it. Then you can work up the line a little so
that every now and then you can sit down for a minute."
This small respite, however, does not free the worker from
the line; like those less fortunate men unable to gain even
this small break, he must be there when the next axle or
motor or chassis or body comes along, as he knows it inex-
orably will. He can only leave the line long enough to go
to the toilet, for example, when a "relief" or "utility" man
replaces him.

The major exceptions to these generalizations are the repairmen and relief or utility men. Repairmen have no fixed,
repetitive tasks to perform. How much work they have to do
depends upon the number of "cripples" (imperfectly assembled units that have not passed inspection) that come down
the line for them to repair. At some times they may work
steadily; at others they may have little to do; and on other
occasions they may have to work under intense pressure and
at high speed. Moreover, each defective unit may require a
different kind of operation, thus providing variety as well as
a greater degree of responsibility. The utility man replaces
each worker for a while in order to give him a brief respite
and an opportunity to go to the toilet. He must therefore
perform a wide variety of jobs on the line, shifting from one
to another in the course of the day. In between each brief

stint he can pause to chat for a moment, if he chooses, or can take a short break from his labors.

Most of the things about which assembly-line workers complain—heavy physical demands, repetitiveness, and the absence of any intrinsic interest or challenge in their work—are also found in many other jobs. But their chief objection, Walker and Guest found in their study of automobile workers, was the distinctive feature of the line, the inability to determine one's own pace or tempo. Only a small minority, usually repairmen or utility men, did not object strenuously to mechanical pacing. Most men found the external, mechanical control of their speed more objectionable than any other feature of their work.

It is hardly surprising, therefore, that there appears to be a general consensus that line jobs are the least desirable in the factory. Walker and Guest report that the workers who had anything favorable to say about the line were usually repair or utility men, both of whom, as we have noted, performed more varied tasks than other workers and were also able to escape more readily from the coerced tempo of the line. In the plant studied by the writer, only sweepers and janitors had a lower standing in the eyes of the workers, and such jobs were usually assigned to older men with high seniority who could no longer perform tasks that required more physical effort. In this plant only one line worker who was interviewed said that he preferred his job to other kinds of routine machine tasks, and none of the men who were not on the line would have willingly accepted assignment to an assembly-line job. Judgments about which departments or divisions of the plant were good or bad to work in were also closely correlated with the presence or absence of moving conveyors at which men had to work.[5]

An English study confirms the low estate of work on the line in the eyes of the workers. In two automobile plants included in an investigation of attitudes toward factory work, boredom and distaste for the job were more frequent and more intense among those tied to a moving conveyor than among others. The amount of dissatisfaction found in the automobile plants was substantially greater than that in a large metalworking factory included in the inquiry. The preferred jobs in the automobile plants were those that had a "longer time cycle," that is, those in which each operation extended over several minutes, and those that required several operations rather than one.[6] As noted earlier, these characteristics suggest less repetitiveness and a somewhat greater likelihood that the worker can vary the tempo at which he must work.

Only by examining more closely what it is actually like to work on the line can one understand why workers dislike so intensely the mechanical pacing that gives the assembly line its low standing among workers. Our evidence, unfortunately and, in view of the symbolic significance of the assembly line, surprisingly, is limited and drawn from relatively few sources, although most of the data appear, on the whole, to be quite consistent. These sources consist of the study by Walker and Guest (the most comprehensive and illuminating of the few systematic empirical investigations of work on the assembly line), my own research, scattered observations in other systematic studies, several analyses of *le travail à la chaîne* by the distinguished French sociologist Georges Friedmann, and a few personal accounts by people who have worked on the line. Some of these sources go back many years—to the 1920's and 1930's; the basic technology has not changed significantly, however, and with due allowance for the differences that might have existed before unionization, even observations made thirty or more years ago remain useful.

Obviously, generalizations about how men respond to the line derived from such limited materials are necessarily tentative and open to serious challenge. As some writers have noted, outsiders may well tend to exaggerate the difficulties of what appears to be onerous and unpleasant labor, and to overemphasize the uniqueness of work on the line. Everyone "gripes" about his job, after all. Why should the complaints of men on the assembly line be taken more seriously, as they may appear to be, than those of other workers? Even the personal experience of those who, like this writer, have worked on the line in order to gain a more immediate understanding, may be of only limited value because of differences between their backgrounds and future expectations and those of most line workers. On the other hand, however, there are also no legitimate grounds for assuming that men can always "adjust" to the circumstances they must live with and that a critical evaluation or interpretation of assembly-line work therefore merely reflects a romantic or "idealistic" response to what are the inevitable realities of an industrial society. That men appear to accept their fate and do not rebel against or even, perhaps, complain about their circumstances may tell us more about the society and culture in which they live than about their experience and character.

The unrelieved and characteristically unchanging tempo of the moving conveyor, the evidence suggests, tends to generate an unusual amount of tension and an urgent, almost explosive, desire for some break in the day's routine. Industrial psychologists have described a "normal" work curve in which output increases steadily during the first part of the day, reaches a peak, and then declines slightly before the midday break; after lunch, output rises again only to fall off as the workday comes to an end. These variations are possible because the worker is able to regulate and control his own rhythm and tempo during the day. The assembly-line worker's output is controlled by the speed of the line, and output is usually constant throughout the day unless the line is forced for some reason to slow down or even stop

for a while. The worker, therefore, may have to begin work
at a faster tempo than he likes, and he must continue to work
at the same speed even when he may want to slow down as
he grows tired or hungry.

At some points during the day, work on the line may
flow freely and comfortably. Even a rapidly moving line can
be handled easily when one is maintaining a satisfying
rhythm of work, and repetitive tasks encourage the establishment of rhythmic patterns of movement. The satisfactions occasionally derived from the even flow of repetitive
work are difficult for men to express or describe, but they
are easily seen or experienced—albeit in perhaps extreme
form—when the tempo of the line catches up the workers in
a state of momentary excitement in which the sheer speed
and movement are satisfying. One morning a woman doing
a small assembly task on a workbench just off the line behind
me, infected by the noise and animation of the smoothly
running line, started to shout in the tones of a circus barker,
"Hurry! Hurry! Hurry!" Walker and Guest quote a worker's
comment: "It makes you feel good though, when the line is
going like hell and you step in and catch it up." And Wessel
Smitter, in his novel *F.O.B. Detroit,* has graphically caught
this occasional excitement and gratification:

The line got into its swing. The fellows stopped joking and talking. There was no whistling or singing or horseplay—no time for
nothing but work. It was good to be back in the noise and the
racket; it was like getting back to city streets after being in the
country a long time. It made you feel good; it made you feel like
you were a part of the factory. On the line there was the rat-a-tat-
tat of pneumatic hammers, the sharp pft-pft-pft and snarl of air
hoses, the whine of electric drills and the hum of power wrenches
and screw drivers. But above it all rise the beat and the peculiar
vibrating hum of the high-speed automatics. The vibrations from
these filled the whole place and got into your blood and your
nerves. It made you breathe faster, work faster; if you wanted to
go slow you couldn't, and if your work didn't keep you busy you

jiggled around on one foot, or made some extra motions with your hands or your arms just to keep in time with the noise. Just to be there—to be making your share of the noise—it made you feel good. It made you feel as though you were a part of something pretty darn big and important.[7]

Such moments, however, cannot last very long; and as the day wears on, signs of tension appear. The only permitted break in the day's work, in addition to mealtime, is provided by the relief or utility man who replaces the worker while he goes to the toilet or simply rests for a few minutes each morning and afternoon. These interruptions, although obviously important, do not eliminate the steady pressure and strain. For example, a man in the line position next to the writer remarked one day in the middle of the morning, "I'd rather be kept busy like this than working too slow." By midafternoon, with several hours yet to go, he repeatedly asked for the time, and commented on how slowly the hours dragged. His face showed signs of increasing strain, and my attempts at conversation brought fewer and steadily sharper replies. Many of the comments reported by Walker and Guest also suggest the strains engendered by the steady tempo of the line:

The work isn't hard, it's the never ending pace.

On the line you're geared to the line. You don't dare stop. The line speed is too great. More men wouldn't help much. They'd just expect more work out of an individual. There's an awful lot of tension.

It's not the monotony, it's the rush, rush, rush.

The tensions generated by the unvarying speed of the line are sometimes further stimulated by the worker's inability to leave his post unless a relief man takes his place. One tough foreman is reputed to have said to a worker who complained because he could not get away from the line

when he needed to go to the toilet, "We don't regulate the
line by your bowels; you regulate your bowels by the line."
Patricia Sexton, a former automobile worker who is now a
sociologist, recently wrote:

In last year's auto negotiations, the fuss about what was euphe-
mistically called "time to perform natural functions" struck most
people as [funny]. But for an auto worker nothing could be so
grimly serious, so brutally basic, as the guaranteed relief time to
go to the toilet. Once an auto worker was fired because, denied
relief time, he went in a barrel near the line.[8]

As tension increases, men begin to look hopefully for an
empty space on the line that would allow them to rest for as
long as their regular task would normally take. If an empty
space does appear, it is greeted with a sigh of relief. Each
time the line's steady movement slows down for a moment,
there is a passing hope that it is stopping. As one worker
remarked to me: "You get the feeling—everybody gets the
feeling and everybody is wishing—whenever the line jerks,
'Break down, baby.' " A study of packinghouse workers reported the same feeling about the moving conveyor. "I wish
a lot of times," one man said to the interviewer, "the damn
thing would break down and you could go home."[9] When
the line does stop, one worker commented to Guest, "We all
yell 'Whoopee.' "[10] On one unusual occasion when the line
on which the writer was working not only stopped but also
backed up for a few feet, the faces of all the men around
me were wreathed in smiles. The line, which had everyone
in its grip, had not only forgotten to be itself but was even
contradicting its own logic.

Yelling itself may provide one way of blowing off steam
during the day. In an impressionistic essay describing life
on the line, a young worker wrote: "Suddenly a man breaks
forth with a mighty howl. Others follow. We set up a howl-
ing all over the shop. It's a relief."[11] A reporter who set out

to refute the impressions of this worker by interviewing men who had been on the line for many years observed the same phenomenon. His explanation for these outbursts, however, is contained in the statement of a worker with long seniority who thought the yelling came from young men simply because they "felt good."[12] It is, of course, quite possible that spontaneous shouting by the workers on the line may on some occasions reflect the momentary excitement generated by noise and movement and on others constitute a release for accumulated tension.

Further evidence of the accumulation of tension can be found in the explosive rush to get off the job at the end of the day. In response to my question, "Is there usually a rush for the time clock when the whistle blows?" one worker answered:

Is there? I usually have about five minutes to wash up and get ready; so one day I was standing about seventy-five feet away from the time clock, and when that whistle blew there were so many men there all of a sudden, you wondered where they all came from. I didn't take two steps before the line was reaching me already. It looked as though they were hiding behind pillars and machines and any place they could to get into the line as soon as the whistle blew.

A similar observation has been made about packinghouse workers who also work on a moving conveyor:

In one of the departments in which the foreman gives a sign when the time has come to leave, the time interval between the sign being given and the room being empty is so short that I did not realize at first how and why twenty people disappeared in an arrow-like fashion within a few seconds.[13]

In many other factories and in many offices the exodus at the end of the day may also be rapid; cleaning up early, clock watching, or waiting anxiously for the bell to ring or whistle to blow are not confined to automobile workers or, for that matter, simply to manual workers in industry. Yet the pell-mell rush for the time clock and the exit observed among workers who spend their working day at the line seemed to this writer and, it would appear, to Fred Blum in his study of packinghouse workers, to be sufficiently explosive to call for special comment as perhaps indicative of greater tension and pressure than that experienced on other kinds of jobs.

So tense are many workers at the end of a day of constant effort at a coerced rhythm that they often find it difficult to relax after they leave the shop. Several workers commented to the writer that after their eight hours on the line they felt it necessary to stop in for a few beers on the way home, and Blum noted the same pattern among packinghouse workers. After being transferred to another job, one worker reported, he no longer felt the need for a tranquilizing drink on the way home. Another man said:

I used to work on the chassis line. When I used to get home my hands would go like that. [He held his hands over the side of the couch on which he was sitting and let them shake helplessly. His wife added: "That's right. He used to be all worn out."] When I worked on the line I felt so bad that when I came home I couldn't do anything.

The wife of a worker interviewed by Guest reported a similar after-work letdown, in addition to persisting signs of tension:

He comes home at night, plops down in a chair, and just sits for about fifteen minutes. I don't know much about what he does in the plant, but it does something to him. Of course I shouldn't complain. He gets good pay. We've been able to buy a refrigerator and a TV set—a lot of things we couldn't have had otherwise. But sometimes I wonder whether these are more important to us than having Joe get all nervous and tensed up. He snaps at the kids and snaps at me—but he doesn't mean it.[14]

The accumulation of tension and the need for a drink in order to be able to unwind at the end of the day are, again, not peculiar to the assembly-line worker, as the numerous descriptions of commuters' club cars testify. The strains of a repetitive job on the line, however, are obviously not the same as those of a business executive or professional performing responsible and prestigeful tasks in a high-powered competitive world. The worker's two beers and the executive's two Martinis differ not only in alcoholic content and status value but also in the problems they are expected to solve and the psychological context in which they are consumed.

Although the evidence thus far presented indicates that workers experience special constraints on the line, there are some observers who have argued that jobs on the line are in fact no different from other repetitive tasks and that most workers manage to adjust to their demands without serious difficulty. Writing in 1931, for example, even before there was a union strong enough to impose some restraints upon management's freedom to set line speeds and determine production standards, Stanley B. Mathewson, usually a keen observer of patterns of behavior among industrial workers, found no signs of excessive demands upon workers on the line:

When one stands on a visitor's bridge at Ford's, for example, and looks down on the beehive of activity below, the impression received is that of tremendous speed. But when one is down there, he soon learns that a rest pause actually exists, in even the most continuous operations. On one occasion I was warned by a fellow worker against a certain job in these words, "Don't go over there —that assembly line is a mad house!" I had heard indeed that that particular assembly process was the "fastest line in America." I begged for a job on that line and got it. To my surprise, I found that in spite of its reputation, the job required only a consistent application of physical energy, not at all beyond my capacity or the capacity of the others about me. In fact, we were a jolly, normal group of workers whose talk as we rode home in a packed bus after eight hours in the "mad house" was never of fatigue or oppression. We kidded each other a lot, and sometimes we wished we could put in six days a week instead of five.[15]

This observation has been widely quoted in defense of the assembly line and as evidence that critics often exaggerate its disabilities. At least as late as 1947, a mimeographed copy was available in the office of a leading General Motors economist to be given to anyone who appeared to be critical of the impact of the assembly line upon workers.

How men respond to the pressures of the assembly line— or of any job—varies, of course, with the personality, previous experience, and present needs and circumstances of each individual. Undoubtedly some men adapt themselves to the mechanically determined pace of work on the highly repetitive tasks on the line. In 1937 a Detroit newspaperman, Christy Borth, reported a number of interviews with assembly-line workers, all of whom had been on the line for many years and did not feel that their work was particularly monotonous or demanding. Men who complained about the line, these workers felt, were simply misfits. "If a man can't get along with his job," one said, "it's not the job's fault I guess; it's the man who is wrong."[16]

Although one cannot casually dismiss these observations, they are not enough to warrant recasting our picture of work on the assembly line or our conclusions concerning workers' attitudes toward it. More recent and more systematic data have revealed clearly the extent to which workers dislike jobs on the line. As noted earlier, most of the workers interviewed by Walker and Guest objected to the mechanical pacing of the line, and 85 percent said that they would prefer more variety in their work. In both their investigation and that of the writer, line workers almost unanimously wanted to secure some other kind of job. Mathewson's observation, it should be noted, came in the midst of the Depression, when any job was highly valued. The threat of unemployment still loomed large in 1937 when Borth reported the satisfaction of old-time assembly-line workers with their jobs. Moreover, one might expect workers with long experience on the line to have adapted themselves in some fashion to their work, while those least capable of adjusting to the line were weeded out. Because some men can adapt to the line, however, does not eliminate its difficulties. The human "misfits," one might argue, are not the men who rebel against coerced rhythms of work and against routine, uninteresting jobs, but rather those who adapt themselves to such circumstances.

A more specific defense of the line comes from those who have seen workers apparently refuse opportunities to gain some variety in their work by rejecting transfers from one assignment to another. Henry Ford once complained that most workers did not want to be moved from job to job, even though, he said, management would be willing to transfer men whenever they wanted to. Stuart Chase remarked, in 1929:

Mr. . . . admits that he too has wept for the soul-destroying effects of the machine and has urged the shifting of men from one routine job to another "to save their tottering reason." Indeed he has tried it in sundry shops—only to be overwhelmed with the resulting riot. The poor slaves did not want to change and said so loudly and clearly. Here was a man lying upon a cradle on his back under the assembly line screwing up a bolt. He had a comfortable position and an admirable rest for his head. When the management threatened to shift his job he threatened to quit. He was convinced he had the softest berth in the shop—"nothing to do but lie down all day and getting good money for it."[17]

Other observers have noted the same phenomenon. The reporter whose inquiries were cited earlier quoted several automobile workers who would have been unwilling to accept a transfer to another job on the line. More recently Georges

Friedmann cites a Belgian clothing firm in which "the girls make difficulties if they are transferred from one assembly line to another, and even occasionally leave the firm if they are forced to change."[18]

As Friedmann notes, however, transfer to another routine job does not necessarily represent an improvement; the girls unwilling to give up their present tasks were usually being assigned to even more limited jobs than those they had been performing. In the automobile industry, shifting from one assembly-line job to another often offers little long-run improvement at the same time that it may, in fact, create difficulties for the worker. Since each job is likely to demand different kinds of movements, and therefore call upon different muscles, the first few days on a new assignment are often accompanied by a good deal of muscular soreness and stiffness. One worker with many years of work on the line commented to the writer:

The first couple of days I was on a new job on the line I used to come home so tired that the fellows used to rib me that I was wearing out the seat of my pants because my ass was dragging so low.

Resistance to changing jobs, therefore, does not necessarily mean that workers are satisfied with what they are doing—or even "adjusted" to it. It may reflect rather an understandable reluctance to undertake the often difficult task of learning a new job that frequently offers no real advantage over the old one. That workers are, in fact, often dissatisfied and eager for more varied, interesting, and meaningful work is evident from the success of occasional efforts to encourage or allow men to learn several routine tasks all of which then become part of their regular jobs.[19]

As a great deal of research has clearly demonstrated, the impact of technology upon workers is always affected to some extent by its social and cultural context. Fatigue, boredom, and dissatisfaction are less likely to appear if men are enjoying satisfying social relationships on the job, both with their fellow workers and with their supervisors. Many of the disabilities of routine repetitive tasks seem less onerous if men feel that their work is meaningful and significant. To what extent, then, is the impact of the assembly line upon workers mitigated or softened by such social or cultural factors?

Assembly-line technology itself often limits the possibility of a satisfying sociability. On the basis of their careful observation in several plants, Walker, Guest, and Turner conclude that "there are fewer opportunities for interpersonal relationships on the line than in less rationalized factories."[20] A few workers are "isolates," physically separated from others—a paint sprayer of wheels and small parts off by himself in a small shed, for example, or a man balancing wheels after tires have been mounted on them, perched on an elevated platform at the very end of a conveyor on which his closest neighbor is at least twenty feet away. Such workers characteristically complain about their jobs, emphasizing strongly the absence of opportunities for social intercourse. On the other hand, a small number of workers actively cooperate in performing some task such as mounting instrument panels too large for one man to handle. As members of a team that is both a "functional and spatial unit," they are able to interact with one another often enough to establish meaningful social relations that can add an important source of satisfaction to the job. But most workers, though in physical proximity to others, face serious obstacles to sociability on the line.

In many parts of almost any automobile plant—and in other manufacturing industries as well—the sheer volume of continuous noise created by moving conveyors, other machines, and power tools makes it difficult to carry on conversation, particularly if men are separated from one another, as they often are, by more than a few feet. Even if there were less noise, the surface mental attention required by many line jobs limits the frequency and extent of interaction with others; workers are simply not able to take their attention away from their jobs long enough to carry on a conversation or do more than exchange a few casual words.

Because most workers, with the exception of utilitymen and repairmen, are fixed to one spot on the line that they cannot leave unless replaced by someone else, their social exchanges are confined to those adjacent to them or directly across the line. Unless a job requires collaboration with others—as only a few do—there is no technical basis for establishing effective social relationships. Nor does the continuous line make it possible to delimit distinctive social groups to which men know they belong. For each man on the line there is a different potential group made up of those next to him or on the other side of the line; no two men are in a position to interact with the same group of co-workers.

Unlike members of functional work teams who often spoke favorably of being able to talk, help one another, or "kid around," most line workers had little "ingroup awareness." "I've been here over a year," said one man interviewed by Walker and Guest, "and I hardly know the first names of the men in the section where I work."[21] This observation echoes those made to the writer by several workers who reported that they had never been able to establish any sort of personal relationship with their co-workers on the line and that at best they enjoyed a superficial, intermittent camaraderie. The occasional—and sometimes frequent—shifting of assignments and of manpower because of absenteeism, quits, or fluctuations in the flow of work further inhibits the development of significant work groups, and increases the tendency toward "depersonalization." Although systematic data collected over a long period of time are not available, the scattered information at hand suggests that the rates of turnover and absenteeism are characteristically higher among line workers than among those doing other kinds of routine tasks. This fact could be both cause and consequence of the inability of assembly-line workers to establish social ties with one another, as well as reflecting the actual disabilities of jobs on the line and their low estate in the eyes of workers.

All the difficulties of the line might be tolerated more readily, even in the absence of satisfying social relations, if men felt that their jobs had some value that transcended or gave significant meaning to their daily experience. Work could have such meaning if men could see their jobs as part of a career in which they could look forward to more interesting work, greater responsibility, and increased income, or if they felt that they were making a contribution to some culturally valued goal.

For most workers, however, there is little opportunity for advancement, and little likelihood that they can view their present job as preliminary to something better in the future. Several studies have shown the limited aspirations and expectations of most assembly-line workers. Whatever interest they express in promotion or transfer in the shop is usually derived more from their desire to escape from the line than from an energetic pursuit of more money or higher status.[22]

Because of the marked division of labor and the concomitant reduction in skill, workers have little sense of a "personal" contribution to a finished product. Keenly aware that they can easily be replaced or readily moved from one task to another, they often belittle the importance of their role in the production process. Walker and Guest remark: "Any production worker can, and sometimes does, say: 'There are hundreds of jobs like mine, not much better, not much worse. The differences are so slight, or seem so slight to management, that I am interchangeable.' "[23] Among the workers interviewed by the writer, "I'm just a cog in the machine" was a frequent theme. The continuing mechanization of production, moreover, poses a constant threat not only to their jobs but also to whatever feeling they might have that their efforts had some social or economic value for society as a whole.

This vacuum of meaning in the job situation is accentuated in the United States—and in most of western Europe—by the absence of a larger set of values from which men can derive some moral substance. As employees of a relatively large, impersonal corporation, most workers seem to derive no immediate benefit from the volume or quality of production. Their efforts and efficiency pay off in profits for the company rather than in greater rewards for themselves. Although this fact need not lead to the class conflict predicted by Marx, it can readily produce a moral detachment from work, particularly when the job itself offers little challenge, and provides minimal intrinsic gratification. (The Soviet Union has tried to avoid this moral detachment, or alienation, from routine, repetitive labor by enlisting workers in the pursuit of large-scale common objectives. Whether they have succeeded—or will in the future—in all likelihood depends largely upon their ability to make workers feel that there is some connection between the achievement of common goals and the satisfaction of private needs and desires.)

Loyalty to a private employer because of good wages, satisfactory working conditions, effective supervision, and long seniority and the assurance of continued employment may lessen workers' alienation from their jobs. Company-organized bowling leagues or baseball teams—or participation in the activities of a trade union—may perform the same function. Yet none of these loyalties or commitments can make up for the absence of meaning on the job or, in the case of the assembly line, mitigate substantially the difficulties it creates.

In a competitive economy, work on the line—and perhaps many other routine tasks as well—has become, in the workers' eyes, primarily instrumental. Its only value lies in what it makes possible off the job. "The only reason a man works is to make a living," said one worker to the writer. "The things I like best about my job," said another, "are quitting time, pay day, days off, and vacations." One makes the best adjustment one can, seeking satisfaction in the things one does after work, resigning oneself to the necessity of routine, uninteresting, and demanding effort in order to be able to support one's family and provide those consumer pleasures so richly available in an affluent society. Wages, as Wilbert Moore has put it, "are less a recognition of merit [or achievement] than a bribery to overcome unpleasantness."[24] In all likelihood, as one finds increasing satisfaction off the job, the less significant, worthwhile, or desirable does the work itself appear. Paradoxically, this alienation from the job is reinforced by the preoccupation with consumption so characteristic of the affluent society the workers' efforts help to create.

The central problem facing the man on the assembly line—and many other workers too—is therefore not one of morality but of meaning. American culture has traditionally viewed work itself as a moral act. Derived largely, although not entirely, from the Protestant ethic, this view, epitomized among workers in the phrase, "an honest day's pay for an honest day's work," could give significance to even the most routine or exacting task. The theological basis for this moral commitment was largely dissolved long ago, but it has been sustained by other forces—economic necessity for both the individual and society, the prospect of gain or advancement, the social aspects of the job. As we have seen, apart from private economic needs, these forces have little relevance for the assembly-line worker. The job has little moral value for him because it has little social meaning. Holding a job remains a moral obligation in America, as well as an economic necessity for most people, but there is now considerable moral ambiguity surrounding the actual performance of the job.

The central moral problems inherent in the assembly line, then, have to do not with the choices and actions of the workers, but with the attitudes and decisions of management and of society as a whole toward work on the line. Technological decisions have social and psychological as well as "economic" consequences, but the technology of the assembly line has been elaborated primarily in terms of economic criteria—efficiency, productivity, cost, and profit. A society with a technology that requires a great deal of strenuous, difficult, and onerous work in order to cope with persisting problems of scarcity is hardly likely to concern itself with the human impact of the tasks that men must perform. In the past—and in all likelihood in the present too—most workers probably have taken for granted as normal or inevitable many of the demands made upon them, even as they have tried to better their working conditions, shorten their hours, improve their wages, and avoid the speedup. The desirability of increasing production has not been seriously challenged, except perhaps by a few advocates of skilled artisanship and rural simplicity. American workers have not been Luddites seeking to destroy the machinery that threatened their skills or their livelihood. They have tried to cushion the impact of technological innovation, occasionally to prevent the rapid introduction of new techniques, but by and large they have recognized the claims of technological progress, and have merely sought to secure more of its fruits.

An affluent society, however, can afford to concern itself in new ways with the human consequences of technology, to make choices between cost, let us say, or efficiency, and the impact of the job experience upon the worker. American industry can now produce an ample supply of goods to meet the needs of most people—if the problems of distribution and poverty can be solved. Indeed, new wants and "needs," it has often been pointed out, must constantly be stimulated merely to keep the economy functioning and men at work. What is produced under such conditions may generate occasional skepticism toward American "materialism" and the value of production itself—and aggravate further the worker's alienation from his job.

Engineers and managers, however, have rarely concerned themselves with the human or social consequences of technology; they have assumed that most workers would perform the necessary tasks, no matter how unpleasant, if they were adequately paid. And, of course, except in periods of acute labor shortage, they have been correct. Proposals to improve or "humanize" work have usually been subjected to an economic test. Rest periods were justified because they would increase output. Effective foremanship that concerned itself with workers' feelings and problems was expected to raise morale and therefore in the long run presumably cut down absenteeism, stimulate greater effort, and thus eventually lead to more efficiency and greater production. Even the introduction of machines that have virtually eliminated the lifting and moving of heavy materials and parts by workers has come about because of the economies they offered rather than because they would lighten the workers' burdens.

It is possible to design technology in relation to human needs as well as according to criteria of efficiency, cost, and profit. On the basis of their research, Walker and Guest recommend various experimental measures that might increase workers' satisfactions: (1) shortening the assembly line and allowing for group control of its speed; (2) creating opportunities for men to "work up the line," to enable them to "vary their pace and 'catch a spell' "; (3) arranging tasks so that there is greater functional interdependence among workers; (4) providing group incentives.[25] The chief aim of these measures would be to minimize the mechanical control of speed and rhythm. Complementing such steps would be a program of "job enlargement" that would seek to increase the number and variety of tasks expected of each worker. This type of program has already been successfully introduced in a few large industrial plants.

The solution to many of the human problems of the assembly line, Peter Drucker suggested shortly after World War II, was "to lay out the assembly in *concept* rather than in space."[26] According to this principle, operations are carefully studied and simplified, but each worker completes the entire sequence required to finish some part rather than merely being confined to only one or a few. On one line, for example, a circular conveyor was used instead of the usual lineal one. This arrangement permitted each worker to move with the line instead of remaining in one place. By the time he had returned to his starting place he had performed a substantial variety of tasks and completed assembly of the part. He could therefore vary his tempo while doing many more tasks than would usually have been possible, work at his own speed (within the limits set by the time required for the entire assembly), and secure the satisfaction that comes from completing a meaningful job instead of endlessly repeating a disjointed, almost meaningless set of motions. Moreover, the structure of the line permitted some increase in the frequency of social interaction, and allowed for the emergence of a clearly defined social group. The result of innovations such as this, Drucker concluded, was "not only a highly satisfied and happy laboring force; there was also an extremely efficient one which produced more than could have been produced on the orthodox assembly line."

As Daniel Bell has pointed out, however, some of the experiments with more "humane" or more "democratic" practice in industry reveal that greater job satisfaction does not always coincide with greater productivity. This fact contradicts the easy, optimistic assumption that enlarging workers' satisfaction is a sure way to more efficient operations and increased profits. The problem, therefore, Bell writes, is:

Should work be organized so as to increase output and decrease costs and—assuming these benefits are passed on—so that there is a larger product for society? Or should work be organized so as to benefit the individuals on the job? Since relative costs are the variables around which our utilitarian calculi revolve, who shall bear the cost, the consumer or the worker?[27]

An effort to design machines and organize production with human needs in mind, therefore, may well require a choice among alternative values and a revolution in the engineer's approach to his task, in management's criteria of judgment, and in the standards of our production-oriented society.

The assembly line, of course, merely poses this problem in extreme form because of its distinctive demands upon the men caught in its grasp. A similar choice may exist in other kinds of work, in which the difficulties are not so pressing as they are on the line. The machine operator also often suffers from the lack of intrinsic interest, the monotony of routine repetitive tasks, the potential moral detachment and loss of meaning in his work. And to eliminate these humanly restricting experiences from such jobs may entail the same choice between economic values and the psychological well-being of the workers.

Eventually, of course, continuing technological progress may solve these problems by eliminating human effort completely; men on the line or at a machine may simply be replaced by new devices or by a totally different technological process. Ford, for example, built a motor plant several years ago that is totally automated, requiring only some technicians to control its operations, and repair and maintenance men to keep the equipment in working order. Some industries have eliminated routine tasks by redesigning the product itself; printed circuits in radio and television sets, for example, have made it possible to dispense with many workers who once performed routine wiring operations. Jobs on the assembly line, however, do not appear to have been changed substantially by the continuing automation of production; the actual assembly process, that is, putting together prefabricated parts into a whole, continues to require the same type of effort and to impose the same harsh demands upon workers as it has in the past.

Even if automation and the introduction of electronically controlled machines should gradually eliminate routine tasks and eventually invade even the assembly process, however, the moral issue posed for modern society by the assembly line will remain: In a society that now possesses—or is on the verge of possessing—a surfeit of goods, shall concern with production and cost continue to take priority over more immediate human values? Our economic calculus has heretofore relegated these values to a secondary place. Not only is there now an opportunity to rearrange these values; there is also an increasing interest in doing so. Students of industry like Charles Walker and Robert Guest, Georges Friedmann in France, and others, often tie their recommendations for humanizing industrial work to an economic rationale, but they have also thrown a new idea into our moral as well as technological and economic consciousness. Their findings and the suggestions they have offered have changed the contours of the problems they have studied. In part as a result of their inquiries, the inevitability of harsh and unpleasant effort in work need no longer be accepted. Now that this traditional view of work—on the assembly line and elsewhere in industry—has been challenged, the way may be open to consider the problems of work from wider and more inclusive perspectives.

NOTES

1. CHARLES R. WALKER and ROBERT H. GUEST, *The Man on the Assembly Line* (Cambridge: Harvard University Press, 1952), pp. 40, 46, 44.
2. GEORGES FRIEDMANN, *The Anatomy of Work,* transl. Wyatt Rawson (New York: The Free Press of Glencoe, 1961), p. 3.
3. *Ibid.,* p. 9.
4. WALKER and GUEST, *op. cit.,* p. 14.
5. ELY CHINOY, *Automobile Workers and the American Dream* (Garden City: Doubleday & Co., 1955), pp. 65–69.
6. J. WALKER and R. MARRIOTT, "A Study of Some Attitudes to Factory Work," *Occupational Psychology,* XXV (July, 1951), pp. 180–191.
7. New York: Harper & Brothers, 1938, pp. 121–122.
8. "The Auto Assembly Line: An Inside View," *Harper's Magazine,* June, 1962, pp. 54–57.
9. FRED H. BLUM, *Toward a Democratic Work Process* (New York: Harper & Brothers, 1953), p. 78.
10. ROBERT H. GUEST, "Men and Machines: An Assembly Line Worker Looks at His Job" (New York: American Management Association, n.d.), p. 6. First published in *Personnel,* May, 1955.
11. GENE RICHARD, "On the Assembly Line," *Atlantic Weekly,* April, 1937, pp. 424–428.
12. CHRISTY BORTH, "Americana: On the Line," *Reader's Digest,* July, 1937, pp. 15–20.
13. BLUM, *op. cit.,* p. 94.
14. GUEST, *op. cit.,* p. 7.
15. STANLEY B. MATHEWSON, *Restriction of Output Among Unorganized Workers* (New York: Viking Press, 1931), p. 151.
16. BORTH, *op. cit.*
17. STUART CHASE, *Men and Machines* (New York: The Macmillan Company, 1929), p. 160.
18. FRIEDMANN, *op. cit.,* pp. 16–17.
19. See, for example, WALKER and GUEST, *op. cit.,* pp. 149–152, and FRIEDMANN, *op. cit.,* chaps. 3, 4.
20. CHARLES R. WALKER, ROBERT H. GUEST, and ARTHUR N. TURNER, *The Foreman on the Assembly Line* (Cambridge: Harvard University Press, 1956), p. 122.
21. WALKER and GUEST, *op. cit.,* p. 77.
22. *Ibid.,* chap. 9; CHINOY, *op. cit.,* chaps. 4–8. See also BENNETT M. BERGER, *Working-Class Suburb* (Berkeley and Los Angeles: University of California Press, 1960), chap. 2.
23. WALKER and GUEST, *op. cit.,* p. 161.
24. WILBERT E. MOORE, *Industrial Relations and the Social Order* (New York: The Macmillan Company, 1951, Rev. Ed.), p. 234.
25. WALKER and GUEST, *op. cit.,* p. 147.
26. PETER DRUCKER, "The Way to Industrial Peace: I: Why Men Strike," *Harper's Magazine,* Nov., 1946, p. 390.
27. DANIEL BELL, *Work and Its Discontents* (Boston: Beacon Press, 1956), p. 44.

3

On the Margin—
The Engineering Technician*

WILLIAM M. EVAN

THE EMERGENCE of new occupations and the decline of old occupations are continuing processes in an industrial society. Stimulated by economic or political developments, or both, the ceaseless process of technological change brings new occupations into being and makes others obsolete. In aggregate and dispassionate terms, the decennial census in the United States records the birth and death of occupations as well as of human beings.

An illustration of the relentless process of occupational and industrial change is the development of the electronic computer after World War II. The rise of the computer industry, producing thousands of different types of computers, called into being a complex of new occupations, including that of the "computer programmer." Simultaneously, it eliminated the need for clerks previously performing, man-

* The author wishes to express his gratitude to Donald G. Marquis for the many valuable comments he made on this manuscript.

ually or mechanically, some of the operations of the computer. Neither the first edition of the *Dictionary of Occupational Titles* (*DOT*) in 1939, which listed over 17,000 occupations, nor the second edition in 1949, with over 22,000 listings, has an entry for a "computer programmer."[1] Undoubtedly, the third and completely revised edition of the *DOT* to be published in 1963—with as many as 6,000 new jobs added—will officially record the birth of this occupation.[2]

Another occupation that does not appear in either of the editions of the *DOT* is that of the "engineering technician."[3] For several decades, the Census has probably classified engineering technicians in the miscellaneous category of "technicians not elsewhere classified." Unlike medical and dental technicians, engineering technicians are comparative newcomers to industry and government.[4]

Along with the increasing magnitude of resources devoted to research and development, the increasing complexity of technology, and the growth in the number of scientists and engineers, the number of engineering technicians has increased steadily. In fact, during the 1950's, this occupation increased more than twofold—from 112,000 to approximately 275,000—which makes it one of the fastest-growing occupations.[5] In spite of the rapid growth of this occupation, the supply has not kept up with the demand,[6] nor has the increase in the number of technicians kept pace with the increase in the number of scientists and engineers.[7] In the opinion of Werwath, a member of the President's Committee on Scientists and Engineers, "it is safe to say that the shortage of technicians is even more severe . . . than the shortage of engineers."[8] Although this manpower problem is not unique to the United States, it is not so acute, as we shall see, in some of the other industrial societies.[9]

In research and development organizations, as well as in manufacturing organizations, the engineering technician has received scant attention by social scientists. In contrast, scientists and engineers have been the subject of several social science investigations.[10] In terms of the occupational hierarchy, the engineering technician occupies a position intermediate between that of the engineer and that of the craftsman or skilled production worker. This position on the occupational ladder and the ambivalent orientations stemming from it tend to make the engineering technician a "marginal man." As in the case of all marginal men, the strains he experiences are mainly social in origin. The major problem facing the engineering technician is the clarification of his occupational identity: he seems to be searching for answers to the questions "Who am I?" and "Who is he?"

The purpose of this chapter is to explore some dimensions of the occupational marginality of the engineering technician, the nature of his occupational role relationships, his relative status profile, his adaptations to role strains, and the sources of some noteworthy cross-cultural differences in the status of this occupation.

CONCEPT OF OCCUPATIONAL MARGINALITY

Before we consider the respects in which the engineering technician is a marginal man, the very concept of marginality bears some consideration. As first introduced in sociological literature by Robert E. Park,[11] and further developed by Stonequist,[12] it referred to a status interstitial between two cultures, whether racial, ethnic, or religious in character. A marginal man is an "individual who through migration, education, marriage, or some other influence leaves one social group or culture without making a satisfactory adjustment to another and finds himself on the margin of each but a member of neither."[13] An example of a marginal man is a recent immigrant to the United States who by virtue of having left his mother country has loosened, if not severed, his ties with his country of origin, and at the same time has not yet become integrated into the culture of the United States. He is a "cultural hybrid," and suffers from anomie, that is, a lack of social bonds and commitments to the norms of a group or a society.

The concept of the "marginal man" has since been applied, by several social scientists, to the analysis of occupational roles. Wardwell, in his study of the chiropractor, argues persuasively that occupational marginality need not necessarily involve an intermediate position between two different roles, groups, or cultures: ". . . there can be marginality to a single well-defined social role. . . . A marginal role is an imperfectly institutionalized one, which means that there is some ambiguity in the pattern of behavior legitimately expected of a person filling the role. . . ."[14] The chiropractor is not torn between wanting to be a physician or, say, a businessman; and he surely is not uncertain as to whether he wants to be a physician or a quack. His role is marginal to the well-institutionalized role of the physician. In other words, marginality may also be used with reference to one role, group, or culture.

There are, to be sure, instances of occupational marginality involving marginality to two roles, groups, or cultures. McCormack, in a study of the druggist, conceptualizes this occupation as one involving a dual- rather than a single-group marginality.[15] The druggist is torn between his commitment to pharmacy as a profession, which involves an orientation of service to clients, and his commitment to pharmacy as a business enterprise, which involves an orientation of maximizing profit from his transactions with his customers. Students of industrial organization have analyzed the conflicting or ambiguous expectations of foremen in terms of the concept of the "marginal man."[16] As the lowest man on the managerial ladder, with meager authority and reward, his identification with mangement tends to be weak; at the same time, he is not likely to develop a strong identification with rank-and-file subordinates who tend to define his role as a representative of management. Similarly, Shepard, in an analysis of occupational marginality of the engineer, conceptualizes the engineer's role as one that borders on the position of the scientist, on the one hand, and on the position of the business executive, on the other. The engineer, in his preoccupation with design, development, or production problems, is concerned with applying an existing body of knowledge to a useful and technically proficient product. Thus, he appears to be alienated from the culture of the scientist which emphasizes the value of contributing to scientific knowledge; similarly, he finds the economic values of the business executive somewhat foreign to him. Hence, he feels marginal to both occupational groups, and they, in turn, tend to reciprocate this feeling of alienation. The scientist tends to scorn him as a "nuts and bolts" man who does not appreciate the meaning of science; and the executive tends to be critical of him as an impractical man oblivious to cost considerations in his work.[17]

Both the dual- and the single-group meanings of marginality are useful ways of conceptualizing occupational marginality. In our analysis of some features of the engineering-technician occupation, we shall alternate, as the data dictate, between a single- and dual-group concept of marginality. Another facet of marginality related to the single-group concept that will inform our treatment of the engineering technician is Merton's observation that a marginal man is one who aspires to membership in a group that denies him admission.[18] This is a central problem of reference group theory: the attitudes of nonmembers—whether eligible or ineligible—toward membership in a particular group.[19]

The engineering technician is a marginal man in that

his occupational life-space is bounded by the engineer on one side, and by the craftsman or skilled worker on the other, and he himself may have ambivalent feelings with regard to either or both of these occupations.

DIMENSIONS OF MARGINALITY

The marginality of this occupational role is reflected in different facets of the structure of the occupation. In considering several features of this occupation, we shall observe three characteristic attributes: uncertainty, heterogeneity, and ambiguity.

Nature of Work. The diversity of functions of the engineering technician is reflected in the multitude of definitions of this occupation. One definition, developed by a committee of the American Society for Engineering Education, illustrates the heterogeneous nature of his tasks:

In general, the engineering technician is a person whose interests and activities are directed chiefly toward the testing and development, the application, and the operation of engineering or scientific equipment or processes. . . . Classified occupationally, the engineering technician performs semi-professional functions of an engineering or scientific nature, largely upon his own initiative and under only general supervision of a professional engineer or scientist.

Typical among the wide array of semi-professional functions performed by engineering and scientific technicians are: Drafting, design, and development of products and of engineering plant; testing, installing, inspecting, operating, and maintaining engineering or scientific equipment; and estmating costs, selling and advising customers on the use of engineering or scientific equipment.

In many instances, the technician may serve as a liaison between the engineer or scientist on the one hand, and the skilled craftsman or layman on the other hand. In carrying out these various activities, he may have group leadership responsibilities.

The technician must be able to communicate mathematically, scientifically, and linguistically.[20]

A summary characterization of the difference between the engineer and the engineering technician reads as follows:

The technician . . . possesses skills which the professional does not usually have. The hallmark of the technician, especially at the higher levels, is his unique blend of some professional knowledge and manual or instrumental skill.[21]

The wide array of functions and qualifications enumerated above suggests that the engineering technician may vacillate between feeling *omnicompetent* and *incompetent* —as good as the engineer, if not better, or merely a "handmaiden" to the engineer. The fact that he is currently doing work engineers were doing twenty or twenty-five years ago[22] and may, in some instances, be doing work indistinguishable from that of present-day engineers,[23] hardly contributes to the development of a clear conception of his occupational identity.[24] No wonder there are differences of opinion not only in regard to the nature of his work, but also in regard to the worthwhileness of his contribution. For example:

Some regard them as "supporting personnel," others consider them as specialists versed in some particular phase of an art or science but lacking, or not being expected to generate, creative thinking with regard to it.[25]

A staff report by the American Institute of Physics extols the contribution of the technician in the following terms:

Behind the experimental physicist in the record of accomplishment in physics stand the instrument maker, the electronic technician, and the machinist . . . often unsung, but not unappreciated in the physics department. One thinks of A. A. Michelson and his instrument maker Fred Pearson, of R. A. Millikan and Thomas O'Donnell, and of Lord Kelvin and C. F. Varley.

Physicists are well aware of the truth of Francis Bacon's remark . . . "The unassisted hand and the imagination left to itself possess little power."[26]

In sharp contrast to this warm praise is the following statement emphasizing the general incompetence of technicians in a research setting:

Instruments and technicians may, I suggest, reduce seriously the creativeness and originality of the young investigator. Before he has had the experience of being a naturalist, a man with his butterfly net, he is cast into a world consisting of a laboratory full of modern apparatus and two technicians who know how to do reliably almost nothing.[27]

Occupational Title. The heterogeneity of the work of the engineering technician is also evident in the bewildering array of titles used to characterize his position. A study of more than 1,000 graduates of the technical-institute program of Pennsylvania State University, classes of 1955–1961, reported over 377 different titles to designate their work.[28] Among the most common titles listed were: design draftsman, electronic technician, laboratory technician, electrical technician, engineering aide, and technical aide.

Such diversity of nomenclature hardly contributes to the development of a coherent occupational identity:

Kinds of work tend to be named, to become well-defined occupations, and an important part of a person's work-based identity grows out of his relationship to his occupational title. These names carry a great deal of symbolic meaning, which tends to be incorporated into the identity. In the first place, they specify an area of endeavor belonging to those bearing the name and locate this area in relation to similar kinds of activity in a broader field. Secondly, they imply a great deal about the characteristics of their bearers, and these meanings are often systematized into elaborate ideologies which itemize the qualities, interests, and capabilities of those so identified.[29]

Two researchers on institutes training technicians conclude that technicians are "handicapped by the lack of uniform titles and credentials which . . . clearly identify their educational background."[30]

Education and Training. The body of skills and knowledge expected of an engineering technician is also ambiguous, in part, because of the variety of educational and vocational routes to membership in this occupation. The majority of technicians have probably obtained their training in an Armed Forces technical school or in an on-the-job training program in industry.[31] A small proportion of technicians may have received some formal education in an evening extension course at a university or through a correspondence course. Probably a minority of the 275,000 engineering technicians have attended a two-year technical institute or junior college.

A survey covering 517 industrial and government organizations employing 287,630 engineers, physical scientists, and engineering technicians found that approximately 25 percent of the technicians were graduates of a technical institute.[32] The quality of these schools varies greatly. Only 38 institutes out of a total of 202 reporting to the United States Department of Health, Education, and Welfare are accredited by the Engineers' Council for Professional Development.[33] Moreover, technical-institute education differs in content and purpose from that of the vocational school, on the one hand, and from that of the engineering college, on the other. As a postsecondary institution of two years' duration, the technical institute emphasizes in its curriculum "the understanding and practical application of basic principles of mathematics and science as they relate to a major technical specialty, rather than the acquisition of proficiency in manual skills."[34]

The diversity in type and quality of training probably

affects the type of occupational self-conceptions developed as well as the type of career aspirations. In the absence of systematic research on this issue, we may conjecture that engineering technicians with a formal education and an Associate degree in engineering from a technical institute will develop hopes for achieving the status of an engineer. A study of students at Wentworth Institute suggests that this may generally be true, at least for students at superior technical institutes. This survey found that 65 percent of the students thought of themselves as "junior engineers," and 84 percent expected to earn the title of "engineer" during their careers.[35] These students may later experience their marginality in that they may perceive their occupation as a transient one and as a stepping-stone to the loftier goal of a career in engineering. To the extent that those with formal training and a technician's degree encounter obstacles to the realization of their career goals, their role strains will probably be considerably greater than those of technicians who have had a relatively informal type of training and who have probably developed different career aspirations.

Rate and Method of Compensation. The shortage of technicians is, in part, reflected in the amount of resources expended by industry in recruiting technicians. The cost of recruiting an engineering technician is almost the equivalent of that of recruiting an engineer. Hence, it is not surprising to discover that there is an overlap in the reward structure of the engineering technician with that of the engineer. The beginning technician's salary may be approximately at the halfway mark on the compensation scale of the skilled worker; and the engineer's beginning salary may be equal to the median salary of the technician.[36] "Sometimes an experienced technician will be paid as much as or more than recently hired engineers, while in other cases, a highly skilled production worker can earn more than a lower level technician."[37] This overlap in reward structure probably engenders some awareness as to the relative standing, prospects, and worthwhileness of the respective occupations. It may encourage some technicians to aspire to the level of reward of the engineer.

Another confusing feature of the system of rewards for engineering technicians is that some employers—approximately three-quarters, according to one study[38]—compensate them on an hourly basis, and some do so on a monthly basis. In other words, some employers choose to treat them as hourly-rated production workers, and others, as salaried engineers and scientists. This, again, underscores the ambiguity as to their location in the occupational hierarchy.

Self-Image and Public Image. Given the heterogeneous nature of the work of engineering technicians, the multiplicity of occupational titles, the varied training and reward structures, we should expect them—as we have suggested above—to differ appreciably in their self-image. Some engineering technicians may be quite uncertain as to how they differ from the skilled worker or from the engineer, and are, accordingly, vague about their career goals. Others may be persuaded that they are more like production workers than like engineers; and some may see themselves as "junior engineers" who will eventually become full-fledged engineers.

The managers of an industrial organization or of a government laboratory employing engineering technicians may have parallel images of members of this occupation. Some may look upon them as potential engineers; others as quasi-engineers with a body of knowledge and skills distinct from engineers'; and still others as skilled workers.[39] Obviously, the fortunes of engineering technicians are in part dependent upon their own self-image, and in part on the image formed by the managers of the organizations in which they are employed.

The public at large probably has a very nebulous idea as to what an engineering technician does, what his career opportunities and aspirations are, and what his relationships are with other occupations. Merritt Williamson, Dean of the College of Engineering and Architecture of Pennsylvania State University, laments, "The public does not know about the engineering technician and there seems to be little desire on the part of high school graduates to consider this work as a possible career."[40] The Census term of "semi-profession," and the designation in some of the manpower literature of "subprofession" to describe the occupation of the engineering technician, highlight the ambiguity of this occupational role. The absence of systematic data on the self-image and public image of the engineering technician is all too evident. The relative frequency of different self-conceptions and public conceptions of the engineering technician, and the sources and consequences of these conceptions, are questions still awaiting research.

Given some of the marginal attributes discussed above, of the engineering technician, how are they manifested in the course of his work-related social interactions?

ROLE-SET INTERACTIONS

In the course of performing his role, the engineering technician enters into relationships with members of various occupations both inside and outside the work organization. This network of relationships comprises his "role-set," which consists of the roles that the occupant of a given status has by virtue of occupying that status.[41] The number of members in his role-set and the degree of occupational homogeneity among them may aggravate or alleviate the marginal characteristics of his occupation. If the engineering technician works in a production, installation, or maintenance setting, he will probably have a larger number of relationships with fellow technicians or with production workers than with engineers or scientists. His interactions with production workers may yield a feeling of *relative gratification* because his job partakes of more white-collar characteristics than does the job of a production worker. On the other hand, if his role-set includes a preponderance of engineers and scientists, he may experience a feeling of *relative deprivation* because of the gap between his semi-professional status and the status of the engineer or the scientist. The latter case is probably more likely to occur in research and development organizations than in any other organizational setting.

If the last assertion is borne out empirically, then it has some implications for the commonly discussed question concerning the ratio of technicians to engineers.[42] The principal concern of those engaged in discussions of this issue is to ensure that there is an adequate supply of technicians in order to prevent the underutilization of engineers. They have not considered the possible effect of increasing the technician/engineer ratio on the conceptions, motivations, and social relationships of the engineering technician. Does *decreasing* this ratio tend to increase the amount of technician-engineer relations and decrease the frequency of interactions among technicians? If this is true, does it have the effect of increasing feelings of relative deprivation? Does *increasing* this ratio have the effect of decreasing the volume of interactions between technicians and engineers and of increasing the frequency of interactions among technicians? If the latter is true, does it have the effect of diminishing feelings of relative deprivation? What effect an increase in the technician/engineer ratio has on the role-set relations of the engineering technician—an empirical question worthy of research—is probably a function of (*a*) the system of allocation of engineering technicians, and (*b*) various social and sociopsychological attributes of the technician, such as his age, training, and career aspirations.

There are at least two systems of allocating engineering technicians in industry: one is on a departmental or "pool" basis, and the other is on a functional or "project" basis. The larger the organization, the more likely it is to use a departmental or pool system. Organizations having a pool system of allocation assign their technicians to projects in which the technician-foreman is the administrative superior of the technician, and the engineer he is working with is responsible for technical matters. Under this system, the engineering technician has two superiors—a situation that may generate role conflict. In a project system of organization, the technician is assigned to an engineer who is responsible for administrative as well as technical supervision.[43] The resulting proximity to the engineer in this situation may engender hopes for some engineering technicians of someday making the transition to engineering.

In an organization that has a pool system of allocation, the technician who has had little formal training, who is in his late thirties, and who has a commitment to his occupational role will probably have frequent interactions with his fellow technicians that, in turn, will probably counteract feelings of marginality.

The social barriers in the relationship between the technician and the engineer are greater, the more inequality there is in the relative status of the two occupations. If the occupational hierarchy in a particular organization is akin to a castelike structure, with the technician rarely making the transition to an engineering job classification, his perceived occupational marginality will probably be accentuated. The experience of the engineering technician as a member of a trade union in which the majority of the members are engineers bears this out. In the now defunct federation of unions, Engineers and Scientists Association (ESA), the dispute which led to its demise revolved around the question of whether the member unions should admit engineering technicians or whether they should be exclusively professional in their membership. In 1957, ESA decided not to admit any other unions that included technicians. It permitted affiliates to keep their technician members but it deprived them of the right to vote on federation decisions. As a result of this decision, some of the member units left the ESA and attempted to form a rival federation hospitable to engineering technicians, "The Engineers' and Scientists' Guild." The consequent weakening of the ESA resulted in its eventual disintegration.[44]

A similar controversy arose in the organization called the Council of Western Electric Professional Employees. The union alleged that management was adding technicians to the bargaining unit in order to dilute the power of the union and alienate engineers from it. Hence, this organization insisted on an exclusively professional association of engineers barring technicians from membership.[45] Such organizational decisions tend to increase the social barriers between the two occupations.

The recent establishment of the licensing agency, The Institute for the Certification of Engineering Technicians, may have a similar effect if it culminates in a separate organizational entity for technicians. Whether the engineering technician perceives the licensing agency as a "segregationist" move designed to block his mobility or as an "integrationist" move promoting his professionalization will probably be reflected in the extent to which he avails himself of the privilege of certification.

RELATIVE STATUS PROFILES

Another way of characterizing the marginality of engineering technicians is in terms of the concept of "status congruency" or "status consistency" and in the resulting types of "status profiles."[47] The occupants of a particular status, such as that of an engineering technician, may be ranked on a set of attributes or "status factors," as Homans calls them.[48] If an engineering technician is consistently high in his rankings on a set of factors, he is obviously more satisfied than a technician whose status profile is consistently low or at the midpoint of the scales. However, if his status profile is inconsistent, with some rankings high, some low, and some in the middle, he tends to feel dissatisfied and is motivated to equilibrate his rankings at as high a level as possible on the various status dimensions.

In all likelihood, the status profiles of engineering technicians differ greatly. To facilitate a comparison between the relative status of the engineering technician and two members of his role-set, the engineer and the craftsman, we shall construct two hypothetical status profiles. With reference to such status dimensions as knowledge, skill, salary, prestige, and opportunity for advancement in an organization, the engineering technician who has a degree from a technical institute and approximately ten years of experience, when compared with an engineer with a degree from an average engineering school and a similar number of years of experience, may have the following status profile:

STATUS FACTORS:	*Knowledge*	*Skill*	*Salary*	*Prestige*	*Opportunity for Advancement*
Profile of Engineering Technician Relative to Profile of Engineer:	Equal	Greater	Less	Less	Less

That the engineering technician is lower than the engineer on salary, prestige, and opportunity for advancement is evident; that he may be higher than the engineer on the skill dimension and equal on the knowledge dimension is not at all evident. His manipulative skills, whether in design, development, testing, assembly, installation, or other kinds of work, are probably greater because they have either been the object of special training in a technical institute or he has had more opportunity to cultivate and perfect them in his work than the engineer has had. Whether or not the two are equal in technical knowledge is dependent on whether the type of engineer we have taken as a subject for a portrait of relative status profiles has kept up with the rapid pace of new knowledge in his field or has obsolesced.[49] If he has obsolesced in his knowledge, there is a tendency for a convergence in the amount of knowledge between himself and the engineering technician. The likelihood of obsolescence of knowledge may be reflected in the leveling of the salary curve of engineers with ten years of experience:

[T]he engineer appears to have lost by his tenth year of employment the salary advantage which he had at the start and which he held fairly well for the first 5 years after graduation. . . . Further evidence indicating that engineers are not as highly paid after 10 years as are men with little scientific and technical training was found in a survey of graduates of New York University. . . . "Engineering graduates in the past decade have enjoyed an everwidening advantage in starting salary. But during this same span of years, however, the gap closes rapidly, and after 10 years, graduates in business and liberal arts and science surpass the engineering graduates in average earning power."[50]

Given a relative status profile, such as we have speculatively drawn above, the engineering technician probably perceives his relative position in the organization as unjust. Under these circumstances, if the organization blocks his mobility aspirations, he probably perceives this as a threat to his status. This is very likely to occur in an organization where the policy is "once a technician always a technician."[51]

In relation to the skilled worker or craftsman, the engineering technician's status profile on the same five dimensions may be as follows:

STATUS FACTORS:	Knowledge	Skill	Salary	Prestige	Opportunity for Advancement
Profile of Engineering Technician Relative to Profile of Craftsman:	Greater	Less	Greater	Greater	Equal

Is the relative gratification he may feel when he compares himself with the skilled worker sufficient to compensate for the relative deprivation he may experience vis-à-vis the engineer? In all likelihood it is not, *unless* he relinquishes the engineering occupation as a reference group. If he should relinquish this reference group, he would eliminate the major source of his marginality.

ADAPTATIONS TO ROLE STRAINS

On the assumption that human beings seek to reduce tensions—a postulate of several social science theories, for example, the theory of cognitive dissonance[52]—how does the engineering technician adapt himself to the built-in role strains[53] of his occupation? If he does not, in fact, relinquish the engineering occupation as a reference group in favor of a craft, there are at least several modes of adaptation open to him.

First, he may engage in "job hopping" in the hope of eventually finding an employer who will give him an opportunity to become an engineer despite the fact that he does not have a baccalaureate degree in engineering. Since a substantial proportion of those reporting themselves to Census enumerators as engineers do not have an engineering degree, this course of action may not prove to be futile.[54] In some companies, labor turnover among engineering technicians, which is generally higher than for engineers, reaches 25 percent.[55] A common reason given by engineering technicians for changing jobs—in "exit interviews"—is "lack of opportunities for advancement." In an unpublished study, 65 percent stated this was a significant factor in their decision to change jobs.

What proportion of engineering technicians, with or without a degree from a technical institute, succeed in becoming engineers in the course of their careers is a question about which relatively little is known.[56]

A second mode of adaptation to role strain—also via a process of search, though it may not entail leaving the present employer—is to find a setting yielding intrinsic work satisfaction and possibly offering other benefits, such as "ultra-clean" laboratories and access to expensive and prestige-conferring equipment, which some employers restrict to engineers only.

A third and related adaptation, also the product of search behavior within the present work organization or elsewhere, is to find a situation that yields an equilibrated relative status profile. This would mean that the engineer with whom a technician is associated is uniformly higher on all significant status factors. When this occurs, the engineering technician will probably tend to legitimize the occupational and organizationally induced differences[57] and develop a cooperative and possibly symbiotic relationship with the engineer, rather than one involving conflict and resentment.

Yet another mode of adaptation entails collective rather than individual action. The engineering technician may join a union of technicians to improve working conditions, though he is unlikely, thereby, to succeed in equilibrating his relative status profile.

A fifth mode of adaptation to his occupational role strains may be via the transvaluation of work values. Instead of yearning for the prestige, autonomy, and monetary rewards that he hopes to derive from the status of an engineer, the technician may seek to realize other work values. One substitute work value is job security. If he obtains a job in a government laboratory or in a large, prosperous industrial organization reputed to have a stable work force regardless of fluctuations in the business cycle, he may find that the benefits he derives from job security are a fair exchange for the work values he relinquishes. Another substitute work value is managerial authority. By aspiring to a supervisory position, whether in relation to other technicians or in relation to other classes of employees, the engineering technician may succeed in achieving an equilibrated status profile relative to another occupational category. In a study of technicians who graduated from Rochester Institute of Technology between the years 1926 and 1952, it was found that 10 percent were engaged in supervisory or managerial work.[58]

A sixth mode of adaptation involves a determined effort on the part of the technician to obtain an engineering degree, even if it means many long years of part-time evening courses. A relatively small proportion of engineering technicians find it economical or otherwise feasible to cope with their occupational marginality in this manner. About 14 percent of the graduates of Wentworth Institute, class of 1961, are in the process of continuing their college education for an engineering degree;[59] 4 percent of the 1962 graduates of the Pennsylvania State University's technical-institute program have chosen this way of solving their occupational problems;[60] and 3 percent of the graduates for the years 1947 through 1950 of ten New York State technical institutes and the Rochester Institute of Technology subsequently enrolled in a college.[61]

These six types of adaptations to the role strains of engineering technicians are by no means exhaustive. Another and obvious alternative available to some young engineering technicians willing to take the risks involved is to leave their occupation for another one. For example, 6 percent of the graduates of the Oregon Technical Institute, class of 1952, reported working in other occupations.[62] Short of permanently abandoning their occupation, those who remain may engage in a number of search operations and experiment with various modes of adaptation in an effort to reduce, if not eliminate, the tensions stemming from a high degree of status incongruency, that is, an unequilibrated relative status profile.

CROSS-CULTURAL DIFFERENCES

A brief cross-cultural comparison of the position of engineering technicians may be instructive from the viewpoint of problems of occupational marginality as well as from general technical manpower considerations.

Although it is risky to compare occupations across cultural boundaries because of the diversity of definitions employed,[63] it has been observed that there is a greater supply of engineering technicians in Europe and in the Soviet Union than in the United States. In terms of technician/engineer ratios, which can be misleading because they may be computed for a company, an industry, or for the labor force as a whole, the overall ratio of technicians to engineers in the United States is approximately 0.32, whereas it is 1.74 in the Soviet Union, 2.42 in France, 2.53 in West Germany, and 4.20 in Great Britain. (See Table I.)

Assuming that the ratios shown in Table I are approximately correct, the variation may be accounted for in terms of differences in the educational institutions and value systems of these countries. In Britain and on the Continent,

TABLE I

RATIOS OF ENGINEERING TECHNICIANS TO ENGINEERS IN
FRANCE, GREAT BRITAIN, UNITED STATES, SOVIET UNION,
AND WEST GERMANY

COUNTRY	REFERENCE PERIOD	NUMBER OF ENGINEERS IN TOTAL LABOR FORCE	NUMBER OF ENGINEERING TECHNICIANS IN TOTAL LABOR FORCE	RATIO OF ENGINEERING TECHNICIANS TO ENGINEERS
France[a]	1954	140,000	340,000	2.42
Great Britain[b]	1959–60	100,800	Not available	4.20
United States[c]	1960	853,738	275,072	0.32
Soviet Union[d]	1960	1,236,000	2,157,000	1.74
West Germany[e]	1956	74,741	189,676	2.53

[a] SOURCE: Organization for European Economic Cooperation, *The Problem of Scientific and Technical Manpower in Western Europe, Canada and the United States* (Paris: Organization for European Economic Cooperation, 1957), p. 76.

[b] SOURCE: The number of engineers in the labor force of Great Britain is reported in Advisory Council on Scientific Policy, Committee on Scientific Manpower, Statistics Committee, *The Long-Term Demand for Scientific Manpower*, cmnd 1490 (London: Her Majesty's Stationery Office, 1961), p. 7. Data on technicians are unavailable on a census basis for the total labor force, but for a sample survey of "engineering and chemical industries." Ministry of Labor, "Survey of the Employment of Technicians in the Chemical and Engineering Industries," *Ministry of Labour Gazette* LXVIII (December, 1960), p. 464. No estimate of the total number of engineering technicians is drawn from the ratio of 4.20 technicians to engineers, found in the survey, for the following reason given in this report: "Because the sample of firms was a relatively small one, no attempt was made to deduce from the results of the survey the total number of technicians of various kinds employed or required throughout the selected groups of industries" (p. 464).

[c] SOURCE: Max Rutzick and Sol Swerdloff, "The Occupational Structure of U.S. Employment, 1940–60," *Monthly Labor Review* 85 (November, 1962), p. 1211.

[d] SOURCE: Alexander G. Korol, "Soviet Research and Development: Its Organization, Personnel, and Funds" (Cambridge: Massachusetts Institute of Technology, Center of International Studies, Working Draft No. D/60-20, forthcoming study sponsored by the National Science Foundation), Appendix A, Table A-1.

[e] SOURCE: Arnold Kramish, "Research and Development in the Common Market vis-à-vis the U.K., U.S. and U.S.S.R." (Santa Monica, Calif.: Rand Corporation, mimeographed, p. 2742, 1963), Table 14, p. 48.

the educational system is elitist in comparison to the egalitarian, mass-educational system of the United States. At
approximately ten years of age, there is a weeding-out process
on the basis of scholastic performance, with the result that a
relatively small proportion of students are eligible for a college education. Thus, for working-class boys in Britain and
in some European countries to attend an institute for the
training of technicians is evidently regarded as representing a substantial amount of upward social mobility. In the
Soviet Union, too, we are told, "To have a son graduate
from a technicum [school of specialized secondary educa-
tion] is a great achievement for a family of modest background."[64] Hence, in these cultural settings engineering
technicians are not as inclined to perceive their occupation
as involving the same extent of marginality that their coun-
terparts in the United States do. The value placed on
achievement and social mobility in the United States appears
to be so much greater than it is in other countries that the
American working-class boy who cannot afford a four-year
college education and who enters a two-year technical institute is apt to feel that he is settling for a "second best"
occupation. Some may rationalize their choice by saying—as
did one student at Wentworth Institute—"The difference
between us and an engineer is that we cram for two years
and they loaf for four years,"[65] thereby asserting, in effect,
that they are the equal of college-engineering students. Small
wonder that in a country like the United States, where
everybody is exhorted to accomplish his utmost and where
there are provisions for mass education at the college level,
it is difficult to induce high school graduates, especially the
majority that do not enter college, to attend a technical
institute. Nor does the widespread "tendency to conceive of
the . . . educational system as a single ladder leading from
elementary school through the university"[66] mitigate the

difficulties of recruiting students to technical institutes. Whereas the United States "produces" about 35,000 engineers a year, the number of yearly graduates from technical institutes is in the neighborhood of 15,000.[67] Instead of producing a ratio of 2 to 5 engineering technicians per engineer, which some educators advocate,[68] we are producing approximately 0.4 engineering technicians for one engineer. In the Soviet Union, there are about 1,200 technical institutes training approximately 225,000 engineering technicians per year.[69] In 1960, according to Korol, the Soviet Union trained 111,000 engineers and 255,800, or 2.3, technicians for each engineer.[70] And to ensure that the graduates of these "technicums" become engineering technicians and not engineers, only the top 5 percent of these graduates are permitted to continue their education for an engineering degree.[71]

In terms of Parsons' typology of social structures[72]— derived from his "pattern variables" which may be interpreted as types of value orientations in a society—in a universalistic-achievement society, such as the United States, it is difficult to motivate people to enter a relatively low-prestige, low-salary occupation, such as that of the engineering technician. On the other hand, in a particularistic-achievement society, such as the Soviet Union, or in universalistic-ascriptive societies, such as Great Britain and some other European countries, the problems involved in recruiting entrants to the engineering-technician occupation are substantially less than they are in the United States.

One direction for coping with the shortage of engineering technicians in the United States is to recruit women into this occupation. The proportion of women in this occupation, though not so miniscule as in the engineering profession, is still very low—on the order of 14 percent.[73] Since there is already a cultural precedent for employing women as technicians in other fields, notably in medicine and in dentistry, the obstacles to extending the practice to this occupation might not be insurmountable. The major source of resistance may be from the engineer himself who, by force of tradition, may prefer to work with male engineering technicians. A corollary problem would be the reluctance of women to enter a predominantly male occupation. Apart from the cultural precedent, which would facilitate the recruitment of women into the engineering-technician occupation, there is a large supply of women who, because of early marriage and the completion of childbearing in their thirties, are prepared to reenter the labor force.[74] Out of necessity, and not only because of their ideology regarding the status of the woman, the Soviet Union has recruited a large percentage of women into the ranks of engineering technicians—approximately 38 percent.[75]

The recruitment of women might go a long way toward reducing the scope of the problem of marginality of engineering technicians in the United States. Viewed as a pre-marriage or post-childbearing occupation, the level of occupational aspirations would be radically lower for women than they are for men. Consequently, we should expect their relative status profiles to be more equilibrated than are those of male engineering technicians.

CONCLUSION

A marginal role, whether occupational or otherwise, frequently is a barometer registering storms, so to speak, in the social system. In a rapidly industrializing society, problems of manning a perpetually changing occupational structure are bound to lead to a considerable amount of role strain. The engineering technician's marginality is a reflection of ongoing processes of change in the occupational structure in response to emerging technologies. Just as craftsmen represent older technologies, engineering technicians may be viewed as representing the technologies of an era of growing automation.

As in the case of other occupations, the clamor for "professionalization" of engineering technicians may increase and take various forms: (a) an insistence on a titular revolution—the standard use of such terms as "junior engineer" or "assistant engineer"; (b) an insistence on formal education in a technical institute or a junior college, and an Associate degree in engineering as qualifications for the standard professional title; and (c) the establishment of an independent association to develop its occupational identity and to protect its economic interests, though not necessarily by means of traditional collective bargaining procedures— in order to avoid the stigma of a manual occupation.[76]

If the pressures for professionalizing the engineering-technician occupation materialize in the United States, then the process of incorporation as a specialty within the engineering profession as a whole might occur. If this were to happen, it would be analogous to the ongoing process to bring the X-ray-technician occupation within the ambit of the medical profession.[77] In general, pressures for the professionalization of the engineering-technician occupation, in particular, and of white-collar occupations, in general, will probably become more insistent in a society in which the *proletariat* is progressively being replaced by an expanding *salariat*.[78]

NOTES

1. United States Employment Service, *Dictionary of Occupational Titles,* Second Edition, Vol. I (Washington, D.C.: U.S. Government Printing Office, 1949), p. xi.
2. A. B. ECKERSON, "The New Dictionary of Occupational Titles," *Employment Security Review,* 30 (February, 1963), p. 19.
3. In a recent supplement to the second edition of the *Dictionary of Occupational Titles,* a new three-digit code has been established for engineering technicians. See United States Employment Service, *Technical Occupations in Research, Design, and Development* (Washington, D.C.: U.S. Government Printing Office, 1961), pp. 97–100.

4. E. ALLAN WILLIFORD, "The Engineering Technician: His Role in Industry and National Defense," *Journal of Engineering Education,* 47
(January, 1957), p. 436; Seymour L. Wolfbein, "Technicians and the
Utilization of Professional Manpower," in National Manpower Council, *Proceedings of a Conference on the Utilization of Scientific and
Professional Manpower* (New York: Columbia University Press, 1954),
pp. 52–55; RALPH S. SMITH, *Engineering as a Career,* Second Edition
(New York: McGraw-Hill Book Co., 1962), pp. 123–124.
5. MAX RUTZICK and SOL SWERDLOFF, "The Occupational Structure of
U.S. Employment, 1940–60," *Monthly Labor Review,* 5 (November,
1962), p. 1210; GERTRUDE DEUTSCH, "Occupational Profile of the Factory Work Force, 1950–1960," *The Conference Board Business Record,*
22 (March, 1963), p. 17.
6. President's Science Advisory Committee, *Meeting Manpower Needs in
Science and Technology* (Washington, D.C.: U.S. Government Printing Office, 1962), pp. 23–24; "Technician Lag Intensifies Crisis,"
Engineering and Scientific Manpower Newsletter, 132 (April, 1962),
p. 1; Board of Trustees, *The Ford Foundation in the 1960's* (New
York: Ford Foundation, 1962), p. 14.
7. JAMES T. BRADY et al., *Teamwork in Technology: Managing Technician
Manpower* (New York: Technician Manpower Associates, 1959), p. 8.
8. KARL O. WERWATH, "Training the Technician for the Engineering Manpower Team," *Journal of Engineering Education,* 48 (June, 1958),
p. 88.
9. EDWARD MC CRENSKY, *Scientific Manpower in Europe* (New York:
Pergamon Press, 1958), p. 156; LEONARD S. SILK, *The Research Revolution* (New York: McGraw-Hill Book Co., 1960), p. 108; ALEXANDER
G. KOROL, *Soviet Education for Science and Technology* (New York:
John Wiley and Sons and Technology Press at M.I.T., 1957), pp. 109–
110.
10. See, for example, SIMON MARCSON, *The Scientist in American Industry* (Princeton, N.J.: Industrial Relations Section, Princeton University, 1960); WILLIAM KORNHAUSER, *Scientists in Industry* (Berkeley:
University of California Press, 1962); ANSELM STRAUSS and LEE
RAINWATER, *The Professional Scientist: A Study of American Chemists*
(Chicago: Aldine Publishing Co., 1962).
11. ROBERT E. PARK, "Human Migration and the Marginal Man," *American Journal of Sociology,* 33 (May, 1928), pp. 881–893.
12. EVERETT V. STONEQUIST, *The Marginal Man: A Study in Personality
and Culture Conflict* (New York: Charles Scribner's Sons, 1937).
13. This is evidently a paraphrase of Park's concept of the marginal man
by DELBERT C. MILLER and WILLIAM H. FORM, *Industrial Sociology*
(New York: Harper & Brothers, 1951), p. 631.
14. WALTER I. WARDWELL, "A Marginal Professional Role: The Chiropractor," *Social Forces,* 30 (March, 1952), p. 340.
15. THELMA HERMAN MC CORMACK, "The Druggists' Dilemma: Problems
of a Marginal Occupation," *American Journal of Sociology,* LXI
(January, 1956), pp. 308–315.
16. See, for example, BURLEIGH B. GARDINER and WILLIAM F. WHYTE,
"The Man in the Middle: Position and Problems of the Foreman,"

Applied Anthropology, 4 (Spring, 1945), pp. 1–28; FRITZ J. ROETHLIS-
BERGER, "The Foreman: Master and Victim of Doubletalk," *Harvard
Business Review,* XXIII (Spring, 1945), pp. 283–298; DONALD E.
WRAY, "Marginal Men of Industry: The Foremen," *American Journal
of Sociology,* LIV (January, 1949), pp. 298–301.
17. H. A. SHEPARD, "Engineers as Marginal Men," *Journal of Engineering
Education,* XLVII (March, 1957), pp. 536–542.
18. ROBERT K. MERTON, *Social Theory and Social Structure,* Rev. Ed.,
(Glencoe, Ill.: The Free Press, 1957), pp. 290–291.
19. *Ibid.*
20. WERWATH, *op. cit.,* p. 880.
21. WOLFBEIN, *op. cit.,* p. 50.
22. SMITH, *op. cit.,* p. 124; MERRITT A. WILLIAMSON, "The Certification
of Engineering Technicians," *Research/Development,* 13 (October,
1962), p. 33.
23. BRADY *et al., op. cit.,* p. 4.
24. HOWARD S. BECKER and JAMES CARPER, "Elements of Identification
with an Occupation," *American Sociological Review,* 21 (June, 1956),
pp. 341–348.
25. R. D. BROWN, "Technicians Increase Professional Productivity," in
*Proceedings of the West Virginia Conference on Utilization of Engi-
neers and Scientists, West Virginia University Bulletin,* Technical
Bulletin No. 49 (November, 1957), p. 18.
26. Staff Report of the American Institute of Physics, "Technical Assistance in Physics in the United States," *Physics Today,* 16 (March,
1963), p. 50.
27. IRVING H. PAGE, "Technicians, Equipment, and Originality," *Science,*
140 (May 3, 1963), p. 451.
28. Pennsylvania State University, *A Preliminary Survey of Graduates of
the Pennsylvania State University with a Degree of Associate in Engineering, Classes of 1955–1961, Their Progress on the Job* (mimeographed, Spring, 1962), pp. 1–4. See also LEO F. SMITH and LAURENCE
LIPSETT, *The Technical Institute* (New York: McGraw-Hill Book Co.,
1956), pp. 80–90.
29. BECKER and CARPER, *op. cit.,* p. 342.
30. SMITH and LIPSETT, *op. cit.,* p. 100.
31. For some relevant data based on interviews with only 15 technicians,
see BRADY *et al.,* pp. 71–72.
32. Engineering Manpower Commission, *Demand for Engineers* (New
York: Engineering Manpower Commission of Engineers Joint Council,
1962), Table VII, p. 49.
33. BRADY *et al., op. cit.,* p. 21.
34. *Ibid.,* p. 15.
35. *Ibid.,* pp. 112, 114.
36. *Ibid.,* pp. 46–52.
37. *Ibid.,* p. 50.
38. *Ibid.,* p. 50.
39. *Ibid.,* pp. 89–90.
40. WILLIAMSON, *op. cit.,* p. 32.
41. MERTON, *op. cit.,* pp. 368–384.

42. See, for example, Engineering Manpower Commission, *Demand for Engineers,* pp. 27–29; H. RUSSELL BEATTY, "The Role of the Technical Institute in the Next Decade," *IRE Transactions on Education,* Vol. E-1 (March, 1958), pp. 24–25; RALPH E. ANDREA, "The Ratio of Support to Professional Manpower in R & D Laboratories" (University of Chicago, Graduate School of Business, M.B.A. Thesis, 1962).
43. N. V. PETROU, "Technicians as an Aide to Engineers," *IRE Transactions on Education,* Vol. E-1 (March, 1958), pp. 26–30.
44. National Society of Professional Engineers, *The Engineer in Industry in the 1960's* (Washington, D.C.: National Society of Professional Engineers, 1961), chap. III; "Engineers and Scientists of America Dissolves," *American Engineer,* 31 (February, 1961), p. 18; KORNHAUSER, *op. cit.,* p. 111.
45. BRADY, et al., *op cit.,* p. 34; T. E. SHEA, "The Implications of Engineering Unionism," *Research Management,* 2 (August, 1959), pp. 149–157; "Western Electric No-Union Vote Hailed by President Mosher," *American Engineer,* 30 (June, 1960), p. 18.
46. Institute for the Certification of Engineering Technicians, *The Certification of Engineering Technicians* (Washington, D.C.: Institute for the Certification of Engineering Technicians, 1962).
47. See, for example, EMILE BENOIT-SMULLYAN, "Status, Status Types and Status Inter-relations," *American Sociological Review,* 9 (April, 1944), pp. 151–161; George Homans, *Sentiments and Activities: Essays in Social Science* (New York: The Free Press of Glencoe, 1962), pp. 91–102; SAAD Z. NAGI, "Status Profile and Reactions to Status Threats," *American Sociological Review* (June, 1963), pp. 440–443.
48. HOMANS, *op. cit.,* p. 95.
49. Cf. WILLIAM M. EVAN, "The Problem of Obsolescence of Knowledge," *IEEE Transactions on Engineering Management,* Vol. EM-10 (March, 1963), pp. 29–31.
50. FRANK S. ENDICOTT, "Trends in the Employment of College and University Graduates, 1959," in National Science Foundation, *Scientific Manpower, 1958* (Washington, D.C.: U.S. Government Printing Office, 1959), p. 12.
51. WILLIFORD, *op. cit.,* p. 437.
52. See, for example, ROGER BROWN, "Models of Attitude Change," in ROGER BROWN, EUGENE GALANTER, ECKHARD H. HESS, and GEORGE MANDLER, *New Directions in Psychology* (New York: Holt, Rinehart & Winston, 1962), pp. 3–85.
53. WILLIAM M. EVAN, "Role Strain and the Norm of Reciprocity in Research Organizations," *American Journal of Sociology,* LXVIII (November, 1962), pp. 346–354.
54. BRADY, et al., *op. cit.,* p. 2.
55. *Ibid.,* p. 40.
56. SMITH and LIPSETT, *op. cit.,* pp. 84–85.
57. WILLIAM M. EVAN and MORRIS ZELDITCH, JR., "A Laboratory Experiment on Bureaucratic Authority," *American Sociological Review,* 26 (December, 1961), pp. 883–893.
58. SMITH and LIPSETT, *op. cit.,* p. 84.
59. Personal communication, Nov. 28, 1962.

60. Personal communication, Feb. 5, 1963.
61. SMITH and LIPSETT, *op. cit.*, pp. 96–97.
62. *Ibid.*, p. 82.
63. Cf. HOWARD ROSEN, "Technicians in the Labor Force of Russia and America," *Monthly Labor Review*, 81 (January, 1958), p. 1; Organization for European Economic Cooperation, Manpower Committee, "Survey on Technicians" (mimeographed, March 27, 1961), p. 5.
64. KOROL, *op. cit.*, p. 110.
65. BRADY *et al.*, *op. cit.*, p. 99.
66. SMITH and LIPSETT, *op. cit.*, p. 3.
67. The President's Science Advisory Committee, *Meeting Manpower Needs in Science and Technology*, *op. cit.*, p. 23; DONALD C. METZ, "Seventh Survey of Engineering Technician Enrollments and Graduates, 1961–62" (mimeographed, April 6, 1962), Table 1.
68. BEATTY, *op. cit.*, pp. 24–25.
69. NICHOLAS DE WITT, *Education and Professional Employment in the USSR* (Washington, D.C.: U.S. Government Printing Office, 1961), p. 190; Engineers Joint Council Delegation to the USSR, *The Training, Placement and Utilization of Engineers and Technicians in the Soviet Union* (New York: Engineers Joint Council, 1961), p. 21.
70. ALEXANDER G. KOROL, "Soviet Research and Development: Its Organization, Personnel and Funds" (Cambridge: Massachusetts Institute of Technology, Center for International Studies, working draft no. D/60–20, forthcoming study sponsored by the National Science Foundation), Appendix A: Tables A-14 and A-15.
71. KOROL, *Soviet Education for Science and Technology*, *op. cit.*, p. 113.
72. TALCOTT PARSONS, *The Social System* (Glencoe, Ill.: The Free Press, 1951), pp. 180–200.
73. BRADY *et al.*, *op. cit.*, p. 52.
74. For a related analysis of the role of women in the engineering profession, see WILLIAM M. EVAN, "Recruitment of Women in the Engineering Profession," *Science*, 125 (March 1, 1957), pp. 387–389.
75. MC CRENSKY, *op. cit.*, p. 157.
76. Cf. NELSON N. FOOTE, "The Professionalism of Labor in Detroit," *American Journal of Sociology*, 58 (January, 1953), pp. 371–380; EVERETT C. HUGHES, *Men and Their Work* (Glencoe, Ill.: The Free Press, 1958), pp. 131–138.
77. Cf. EDWARD GROSS, *Work and Society* (New York: Thomas Y. Crowell Co., 1958), p. 223.
78. Cf. DANIEL BELL, *Work and Its Discontents* (Boston: Beacon Press, 1956), p. 50.

4

In the Courts of Power—
The Advertising Man

IAN LEWIS

ADVERTISING, MORE than any institution in contemporary
society, is a cynosure. It symbolizes and concentrates in its
image all that is considered both good and bad in present-
day commercial and industrial capitalism in America. The
importance attached to advertising by laymen, by businessmen, and by advertising men themselves far outweighs its
numerical importance. Only 60,000 people are directly employed in advertising agencies in this country, a small number compared with, let us say, the number of doctors
(235,000), public school teachers (1.6 million), or plumbers
(300,000).

Nevertheless, advertising men do have important economic functions. In 1962 about $12.2 billion was spent on
advertising. This money was actually spent by American
businessmen, not by advertising-agency executives. Advertising men at the most consulted, recommended, and advised
businessmen on this expenditure. Only a small part was

directly spent by advertising men in the preparation of print advertisements, TV and radio commercials, car cards (advertisements on buses, subways, trains, and trucks) and on billboards. For advising on the total expenditure and for preparing these advertisements, advertising agencies received commissions that are approximately 15 percent of the total outlay by the clients. Thus the net commissions of advertising agencies are approximately $800,000,000, which, compared with the size of the gross operating income of the automotive industry ($10,000,000,000) or of the steel industry ($8,000,000,000), can only be described as small potatoes.

Yet advertising as an industry is as much a cynosure for American society as is the automobile industry or the steel industry. This is because these are basic industries (with some exception taken to amount of waste in the design and the annual turnover of automobile models), while advertising is a controversial issue and institution in American society.

At the simplest levels, academic, aesthetic, intellectual, and cultural leaders continuously attack advertising for being the source of all of the moral, cultural and intellectual depravity and bad taste in American mass media. Such an attack overstates the cases because, in the first instance, advertising men only recommend the shows, programs, and placements of advertising to their clients. The final responsibility rests with the client, but when criticism is made, advertising men are the public scapegoat. They are paid to be so, and many wish that they had the actual influence or power that the critics attribute to them. Advertising is charged with stressing only the material, sexual, and vulgar lower values in the human personality. It is charged with stimulating the sense of individual inadequacy by reminding individuals of their imperfections and their unattained goals, and in raising hopes for the achievement of unattainable goals.

At a more sinister level, advertising men are attributed the powers of a Svengali, the sinister *deus ex machina,* that by devious and highly developed psychological, linguistic, and artistic devices brainwashes the American public. It is charged with controlling the foci of the public's attention, feeding the public lies and operating on its unconscious and irrational faculties so that people cannot make rational decisions. In fact, the most serious charge made against advertising is that it destroys the capacity for rational behavior, makes men infants, and by creating these habits of thought destroys the psychological and intellectual capacity for democratic decision-making and for self-government.

As compared with the severity of this charge, direct or indirect charges aimed at the media-selection functions of advertising appear to be secondary. Advertising men, insofar as they are advisers for their clients, are charged with bringing about the demise of numerous magazines and of weakening the strength of independent newspapers and radio as media, simply because their impersonal concern (correctly or incorrectly assessed) for economic efficiency has resulted in the shift of much agency advertising money (34 percent) to television. Whether advertising agencies had the power to make these decisions, or whether the decisions made were simply objective recognition of inescapable facts, is for the moment beside the point. What is central is the fact that advertising is the object of scorn and criticism for possessing in a high degree precisely those characteristics for which our entire society is criticized.

In a peculiar way, however, advertising men are romanticized and envied for possessing the same characteristics that are criticized. They are seen as supermen or super-idiots who live in Ivy League or "gray flannel" suits. They are pictured as leading glamorous lives over expensive lunches, entertaining either fatuous or overdemanding clients, and indulging in sexual promiscuity for business reasons or as

an escape from the frustrations of business. They are de-
cribed as leading barren but exciting lives in suburbs or
exurbs, with alcohol and their own and other people's wives,
neglecting their children and, by ill-thought-out political
gestures, upsetting the politics of their sterile but expensive
communities.

Advertising men are articulate, and do not take their
criticism in silence. They add to the controversy by attack-
ing the long-haired, irresponsible, negativistic, brainless
professors, aesthetes, and faggots who never met a payroll
and who would undermine the American way of life out
of envy of the success of their superiors.

They answer the specific charges by "proving" that advertising provides an essential function for an ever-expanding
American economy by stimulating new needs and new wants,
which only an expanding industry can satisfy. It accelerates
the process of "creative destruction" which, in Schumpeter's
terms, provides capitalism with its dynamism and growth.

Advertising, it is asserted, creates markets for new products and expands the markets for old ones. It forces the
research and development departments of major manufacturers to experiment continuously and to achieve scientific
miracles that enable one competitor to raise the quality of
its brand over that of another. For advertising, the argument
goes, is the soul of competition, and competition is the
heart of American enterprise and its free enterprise economy.

On the cultural front, advertising via the mass media is
allegedly an important vehicle for the dissemination of serious culture and political awareness. Advertisers support,
when it is economically feasible, the production of Shake-
speare on radio and television, the ballet, the symphony,
and the opera on television, together with news programs,
documentaries, and "specials." Moreover, advertisers support newspapers and serious magazines, as well as entertainment in magazines. And, finally, they make it possible, it is

reasoned, for newspapers to educate and inform the American public.

Advertising per se informs the public, the argument continues, of the range of brands available, provides information as to the virtues of these brands ("You can't expect advertisers to knock their own products") and makes it easy for individuals to make "consumer choices."

We expect the controversy to continue indefinitely, to wax and wane, as journalists, moralists, politicians, and intellectuals mount new attacks and are repulsed, or when the issues die for a time because of the exhaustion of the protagonists and of a weary public to whom all of the words are too familiar.

The controversy over advertising and advertising men will probably never be resolved at the ideological level. Nor can advertising be understood at that level. Advertising is an industry, composed of separate firms, agencies, each of which has a highly organized internal structure and distinctive but not uniform methods of dealing with its separate clientele, subsidiary organizations (media agencies and subcontractors), the government, and the public. Surrounding the individual agencies are associations of advertising agencies (the "four A's"—Association of Advertising Agencies of America—the Advertising Council, and professional associations composed of the respective technical and professional specialists, employees of a wide variety of agencies). To complete our schematic outline, there are personal and informal cliques that make up a series of interlocking friendship and acquaintance patterns that cut across agency lines, departmental lines and, in some cases, client, agency, and subcontractor lines of communication.

In all the above formal respects, the advertising business does not differ from other businesses. Our discussion will therefore be confined to those aspects of the advertising business that are either unique or that are accentuated much more than is usual in other businesses. We shall, therefore, describe the structure of the advertising industry in order to set the stage for a more detailed discussion of advertising as a drama in which some of the ethical and moral dilemmas at work in our society are acted out.

ECONOMIC AND STRUCTURAL CHARACTERISTICS OF THE ADVERTISING AGENCY

1. Advertising is a labor-intensive and capital-extensive industry. The advertising agency makes no great investments in capital goods. Its major capital investments are in typewriters, calculating machines (and in a few large agencies the rental of computers), duplicating equipment, and office furniture. The rental of office space is the major fixed cost of an agency. By and large, labor costs—primarily salaries—are the single largest item in agency costs. Labor costs on an average constitute 70 percent of the annual operating costs of an advertising agency.

Because of the absence of an elaborate machine technology and the corresponding presence of labor-intensivity, advertising is properly called a service industry. Advertising men emphasize this service feature of the agency until the truth becomes a cliché. The composite cliché is as follows: "All we have to offer our clients is a service—our skill, our knowledge, our brains, our talent, our know-how, and our judgment. All we create are ideas, plans, slogans, and arrangements of words, pictures, sounds, and symbols. To the extent that we execute these functions well, and only to the extent that our clients have need for these functions, are we entitled to the high fees, commissions, and salaries we earn."

If an agency can succeed in convincing a prospective

client that these claims are true (and they are claims until proved or disproved by subsequent actions), the agency can make a powerful case. For American business has a continuous need for "brains," ideas, judgment, wisdom, counsel, and know-how. It is by now a truism that most major brands of consumer goods are not distinguishable from one another to the consumer when he tests them by means of blind-product tests. If this is true, the tremendous differences in the sales success of various competitive brands are primarily due to differences in the marketing effectiveness of the competitive manufacturers, including advertising.

In a number of industries the marketing organizations of the manufacturers (the sales and distribution organizations, the financial reserves, the dealer-relations programs, merchandising and sales-promotion programs) are considered to be at a parity. However, some companies have made tremendous sales successes with the introduction of new brands and the revitalizing of declining brands, while the equally well-marketed competitive brands (aside from advertising) have suffered declines or only moderate gains in sales.

Thus a slogan like "Winston tastes good like a cigarette should" or "Be sociable, have a Pepsi," have been worth hundreds of millions of dollars to their respective manufacturing companies.

However, since the advertising agencies' claim for their value to business is based on the intangibles of skill, talent, knowledge, know-how, and so on, and not on objective technological processes, the client can at any time reject the claim, especially since every advertising agency makes substantially the same claim in attempting to seduce accounts from other agencies.

2. While we have stressed the fact that the operating income of agencies is relatively small, the number of persons engaged in advertising is still smaller. The labor-intensity

of advertising thus consists of a relatively small number of highly paid specialized technicians and managerial officials.

A large-sized but not gigantic agency with billings of approximately $100,000,000 will have an operating income of $15,000,000. If we allow all costs but labor costs and profits not to exceed $3,500,000, then direct and indirect payments to personnel will amount to $11,000,000. Such an agency, if well run, may employ from 600 to 700 people. The average agency income available for profits and payments to personnel is thus in the neighborhood of $16,000 to $18,000 per employee. Since at least 60 percent of the employees of an advertising agency are relatively low-paid clerical, bookkeeping, and stenographic help, the average amount of money available for the professional, creative, and managerial staff is estimated at (depending upon whether the agency employs 600 or 700 persons in total) from $27,000 to $34,000 per professional employee. Since many agencies are owned by their professional, creative, and managerial staffs, salaries, profits, and profit-sharing funds can at times be considered as part of the same pool.

Of course, not all agencies are so profitable as our hypothetical but not improbable agency. And, of course, we have been dealing with averages—averages in salaries and an equal distribution in stock throughout the professional staff. Both of these assumptions are contrary to fact. There is great range in the salary levels of various professional, creative, and managerial officials of an agency. And even while many agencies are "employee-owned," the chief officers and executives are likely to own the lion's share of stock, with middle- and lower-level officials owning just enough to satisfy the Bureau of Internal Revenue (that the company is employee-owned and not a proprietorship) and the implicit or explicit demands of these lower-ranking officials for equity. These latter demands are granted either to keep valued employees happy or to seduce them from a competitive agency.

Table I indicates the average salary range of a number of typical positions in a relatively large advertising agency, according to the director of the largest employment agency servicing the advertising business:

TABLE I

Account Supervisor	$30,000–$40,000
Account Executive	$15,000–$25,000
Asst. Account Executive	$ 6,000–$12,000
Merchandising Director	$25,000–$35,000
Asst. Merchandising Director	$15,000–$20,000
Market Research Director	$20,000–$40,000
Media Director	$20,000–$40,000
Media Buyer	$10,000–$15,000
Junior Media Buyer	$ 5,200–$ 6,500
Creative Director	$25,000–$60,000
Copy Chief	$35,000–$45,000
Copy Supervisor	$25,000–$35,000
Copy Group Head	$18,000–$30,000
Copywriter	$ 8,000–$18,000
Head Art Director	$30,000–$45,000
Group Head Art Director	$20,000–$25,000
Art Director	$12,000–$20,000
Art Director (Board)	$10,000–$15,000
TV Art Director	$15,000–$25,000
TV Story Board Artist	$ 8,000–$12,000
Production Manager	$12,000–$18,000

Salaries, per se, cover only part of the perquisites of the advertising man. Profit-sharing plans allow the agency official to accumulate a retirement fund or a separation allowance that may result in a yearly deferred income of up to 20 percent of his annual income, which when collected is taxable at capital-gains rates.

Stock options and increases in the value of stock in the agency (whose prices are artificially pegged by the company) provide additional capital gains. The opportunity to acquire stock, however, is more than a capital gain, a way of evading taxes when one moves up the income ladder. Stock acquisition is a genuine method of becoming wealthy, based on talent alone, as the agency defines talent. Since the advertising agency is a capital-extensive and labor-intensive industry, the physical assets of an agency do not constitute a limit to stock acquisition. One does not "water" the stock (physical assets) by issuing more stock (equity shares), since the physical assets are of little value in themselves. The issuance of stock to an individual simply means that his "services" represent an important part of the service that the agency sells to its actual or prospective clients. Of course, if an individual makes known to his bosses his estimate of his own worth, they are more likely to calculate the value of that individual's services in terms of the total matrix of the agency's total income-earning services, and reward him accordingly.

All of this means that valued individuals can easily acquire stock, and can do so at a very young age. Stock acquisition is made easy by issuance of new low-price issues, by options, and by deferred-payment plans. The ease of stock acquisition means that in advertising, the American dream of rags-to-riches can be realized in a sufficient number of cases to serve as goad and pull to thousands of young men in advertising who may be on the make.

That the agency president and majority stockholder of a $100 million (billing) corporation is the son of Italian immigrants, or that another may be the son of a Jewish rag buyer, is both a reality and a myth. The reality is one that can be illustrated by thousands of examples, and everyone in the advertising business has his own favorite illustration. The use of this reality becomes the myth for these thousands of others, and enables them to sustain the pace that advertising demands of them.

The countermyth that advertising opportunities are reserved for "bright" young men from Ivy League schools is also true, but less true. Bright young men from Ivy League schools are especially valued to the extent that their lack of enough imagination to know the difficulties inherent in their work enables them to act with poise, confidence, and with sufficiently good manners as to charm and gain the confidence of clients. Such charm, poise, self-confidence, and manners are as important as skill and talent in gaining and retaining clients.

Despite all this, the agency approach to rewarding its personnel is to reward those whom it must (nothing is given away) for whatever talents appear to be necessary. Thus Ivy Leaguers and non–Ivy Leaguers, Catholics and Jews are rewarded. Since a wide variety of types of ability can be used to justify an agency, a wide variety of talents is rewarded. On the whole, this works in favor of the able, regardless of origin.

Becoming a millionaire is thus the major promise that the myth of advertising offers to the able. It is not the only promise. To those who know they will be moderately successful but will not become wealthy the opportunity to live as if one were rich is almost as seductive. This is done through "fringe benefits."

Advertising men are the customers of the media representatives (television and radio networks and stations, newspapers, magazines, and outdoor advertising), of television and commercials production companies, of graphic-arts firms, of research firms, and of thousands of would-be suppliers of services. The standard way of selling one's services is to wine and dine the agency repreentative who is reputed to have even a minor voice in a "buying decision." Thus an agency official (in New York) with an $8,000-a-year salary, or more, will be wined and dined at one of the hundreds of "expense accounts" restaurants or hotels. He will eat and drink at the Plaza, the Waldorf-Astoria, the Commodore, the New Yorker, or the "21" Club or the Stork Club. If he is deemed really important, he then receives the supreme accolade by dining at the Chambord, the Four Seasons, or the Forum of the Twelve Caesars. The ubiquity of the free lunch reflects the lack of centralization in advertising. Almost anyone can influence the buying decision. In manufacturing, purchasing is centralized.

At the same time that he is being wined and dined, the agency official may read magazines that come by free subscription, drink whiskey that is part of his Christmas loot, or present his children with toys that are given to him as promotion pieces to advertise a product. If the agency man is truly unscrupulous, and if he has or can convince a prospective supplier that he has great buying power, the gift he receives may be a car, a boat, a European vacation, or sexual access to starlets, models, or television beauties. The public image of the advertising man is not entirely wrong.

The other side of the wining-and-dining complex is almost equally attractive (if one is attracted). The agency man is the supplier for the advertiser to the client. As such, his job is to wine and dine the client. Everything that advertisers do for the agency man can be and is done for the client. There are some differences, however. The amount spent on entertainment is expected to be appropriate both to the position of the agency man and to the position of the entertainee in the client organization. One is not expected to take a "clerk" to the Chambord, nor is a "clerk" expected to entertain the president or the advertising manager of the client firm. If he does, he appears to be arrogating the position of his bosses.

There are other differences. When entertained by the suppliers, a low-level agency official can be gay, carefree, and expansive, even to a high-ranking official in the supplier firm. When he entertains the client, a high-ranking agency man must, if necessary, pretend deference even to a low-ranking official in the client firm. Thus mobility in temperament becomes a role requirement for the advertising man.

The expense account thus becomes a major way for a man of modest income to live, during the day, as if he were rich. And this quality of life is far more important psychologically than any increment in income the agency man can gain by cheating on the expense account.

There is some prestige attached by one's peers to having a legitimate reason for eating "for free" frequently; and peers will "keep score" on the size of the tab and the number of times one does so. For agency men accept the myth of the glamour of advertising as much as does the lay public. The poignancy of this acceptance is illustrated at the time when the luncheon appointment is canceled at the last moment and the agency man finds himself eating hamburgers at Nedick's instead of *pâté de fois gras* at the Chambord. (No discussion will take place here on the response of the wife who, after preparing a fancy dinner, discovers that her husband is not hungry because he has had a three-hour lunch at the Chambord.)

We have described the favorable economic and romantic myths and realities surrounding advertising that spring essentially from its labor-intensity. The economic disadvantages also spring from this labor-intensity. Whenever an agency loses an account, or whenever it is deemed necessary to cut operating expenses, the largest single pool of expenses is the pool available for salaries and wages (since over two-thirds of all agency expenses are in this category). Similarly, since the major concentration of labor costs is the high salaries offered to creative, technical, and managerial staffs, the major opportunities for cost-cutting are in this area. To state it differently, firing clerks and secretaries to cut costs is not particularly effective, since the salaries of these categories do not contribute much to costs.

This potential vulnerability of the upper management in the agency business is from time to time made an actuality when accounts shift. The agency that loses a major account (from $2,000,000 to $25,000,000) finds itself in a cost-income squeeze. If the account lost represents a sizable proportion of its billings, the other accounts cannot bear the burden of maintaining the salaries of the executives. Wholesale firings are likely to ensue. However, since many account personnel work on more than one account, if they are fired because of the loss of one account they are unavailable for work on other accounts. The clients of these other accounts may resent the loss of favored copywriters, account executives, commercial producers, or media planners, and take their accounts out of the agency. Thus the loss of one major account may start a vicious cycle that in a number of specific instances has resulted in the sudden demise of large and profitable agencies.

Account shifts in the agency business are fairly frequent. In 1961, 260 accounts shifted, representing $322,000,000 of billings, and approximately $48,000,000 in commissions. The loss of a $2,000,000 account is likely to result in the loss of ten jobs with an average salary of $20,000 (unless these jobs are absorbed by other accounts in the agency losing that account); the loss of a $25,000,000 account is likely to lead to the loss of 188 jobs (assuming the same conditions).

When such losses occur, the job market becomes flooded with applicants, including many individuals who have the same general qualifications. Whether such enforced mobility constitutes an asset or a liability to the career aspirations of an individual depends on the opportunities available at the time of loss of job. In advertising, the loss of job by competent, capable, and blameless men constitutes a major career obstacle.

Theoretically, when an account shifts, just as many new jobs are created as are lost. This is not true in fact, since the agency to which the account shifts will attempt to maximize profits by "doubling up," using hitherto untapped "capital resources" before it employs new people.

Moreover, even if an agency has to "staff up" to absorb a new account, the permanent staff of that agency will view the new acquisition as an opportunity for advancement to new positions, new titles, and salary and stock-acquisition benefits. It is for this reason that the individual who had a good position with the agency losing the account is not likely to be desired by the agency gaining the account. Moreover, since an account shifts because the client is "unhappy" with his former agency, the most visible officials in the losing agency (with some exceptions) are likely to be *persona non grata* to the client and thus to the gaining agency.

Thus it frequently happens that precisely those people who have been most successful in the past, and who appeared to be most worthy of the high salaries they were earning prior to the involuntary loss of job, have the most difficulty relocating. As a result, every individual in advertising knows a person or knows of a person who was "near the top" who has become unemployable through no fault of his own. Such individuals may go into the consulting business, sometimes profitably and sometimes using the fiction that being self-employed justifies the absence of any substantial income. Others retire at young ages and live modestly off the gains from profit-sharing plans and the capital gains from the forced sale of their stock in the company that let them go. Still others become stock and mutual-fund salesmen or real-estate agents, attempting to sell to their former colleagues.

Some, the younger ones, may become schoolteachers—a profession that is continuously enriched by talented, able, but unfortunate victims of the economics of the mass media. A few go into family businesses, if they are fortunate enough to have a family business. Some relocate at salaries that may range from one-third to one-half their former salaries, and these may recoup their losses if they do not become embittered in the process. Some, especially if their skills are in the creative departments (art, copywriting, musical composition, and so on), may shift jobs without penalty.

Thus the great opportunities in advertising are offset by the equally great opportunities for total defeat and loss. A job on Madison Avenue appears to be a game of chance, perhaps roulette, or even Russian roulette. In fact, for a time the phrase "Madison Avenue Roulette" meant that the last man to lose his nerve was the man who would win. A job on Madison Avenue is a Tontine, a last-man's club, where the victims are the living dead, embarrassing reminders that "it could happen to you."

The atmosphere of gambling that characterizes all aspects of the agency business is reinforced by the defenselessness of the agency and its personnel in the face of the whim, fancy, and even perhaps of the wisdom and ability of the client. This ambiguity is the opposite side of the coin from the confidence, assertiveness, and brazenness that advertising men exhibit in making a pitch, when they claim that advertising can do anything and everything.

The ambiguity that represents the greatest opportunity and menace for a specific agency is simply based upon the inability, in all but extreme situations (as previously specified), to measure the value, efficiency, and effectiveness of a specific advertising idea, advertisement, or campaign. Sales may go up fantastically, and sometimes both the agency and client may be in a frenzy to know why. This becomes a problem because, if one does not know what one is doing to make sales go up, any change may be disastrous. Second, if one's gains are thought to be due to chance, then chance can convert the gains just as easily to losses. Similarly, sales losses do occur even after it appears that every step taken by the agency and the client has been thought out carefully, planned, researched, and pretested, and when all concerned have been convinced they have a winner.

The "irrationality" of the marketplace is a source of anxiety, despite the fact that every step may be taken to rule out chance. Research, surveys, pretesting, test markets, controlled experiments—all are attempts to eliminate this ambiguity and irrationality. But the failure to anticipate, to prevent one's "best laid plans" from going astray, is part of the very structure of the market. So many things go into the marketing operation, of which advertising is only a small part, that it is almost impossible to isolate the contribution of a single commercial, slogan, campaign, piece of artwork, or media plan. One can specify all the factors that might conceivably lead to sales success, but one recognizes that each factor applies to one's own brand and one's own marketing operation (including advertising) and also applies to each of a dozen competing brands and to each of a dozen product classes that do not compete directly but do constitute substitute methods of consumer-income disposal. Thus, a brand of beer may compete with all other brands of beer in its sales area (though all brands do not compete uniformly throughout the entire sales areas), with whiskey (by brands and types), with income that might be for the children's shoes, with other types of entertainment, and with, as in the case of shoes, other brands and types of necessities.

For each competitive situation, then, there may be several hundred factors that affect the success of the advertised brand. Several thousand factors, therefore, may affect sales success. As if this were not bad enough, it is almost impossible to isolate each factor as it operates in the marketplace. The marketing operation is so complex that each factor is simply one small element in a causal chain, but unusual success or failure in any one factor can affect the total chain.

A further complexity is introduced by the fact that it is extremely difficult to measure each factor separately or to measure two or more factors together in terms of a common scale of values. In the latter case, it is as difficult to measure the relative importance of each factor as it is to measure the factors themselves. Moreover, the factors involved in any "marketing chain" are continuously changing. Each successful or unsuccessful attempt at measurement may become ancient history before the measurement is completed.

All research—marketing, sales, copy, product, package, consumer, motivational, media, merchandizing, test-market, image, and operations research—represents attempts by the client or agency to narrow the ambiguity or to reduce the risk in making decisions. And all these methods must confront the difficulties of action in a complex "irrational" and uncontrolled market for which there are limited and imprecise measures. Over $100,000,000 is invested in marketing research in one year by agencies and by clients in their anxious attempts to overcome the irrationality of the marketplace.

The feeling of anxiety and powerlessness held by top executives in the face of the tremendous responsibilities placed upon them for sales and advertising success constitutes the largest single opportunity for both missionaries and charlatans in the field of advertising research. There is a cycle in research that begins when a "charismatic" hero discovers a new approach—the large-scale sample survey, program analyzing, the store audit, image research, motivation research, operations research, semantic differential, scale, scaling research, computer simulation, or linear programming, to name a few. After each such "discovery," there is an intensified assault on sales resistance of top agency and client officials, which proves conclusively that once the new method is adopted, rationality and "science" will govern marketing. Many of the methods and services are "bought," and the new crusade begins. After the results of such research are in, the method is either discarded or absorbed as a minor tool in the inventory of available methods for research. The method, when absorbed, develops its defenders, who now resist the claims of new crusaders who possess another final solution. The failure of such methods to allay the sense of powerlessness and anxiety in the face of an irrational market is attested by the fact that each new discovery is superseded by a newer one which, in time, will be superseded.

This does not mean that research methods are universally useless. It does mean that, in the light of the complexity of marketing, research works best when there is a clearly defined, specific problem which can be so stated that a specific research finding can, in advance, be interpreted as offering a solution to the problem. Thus small, undignified, and inelegant studies frequently are the most useful, simply because there was a reason for undertaking them. However, these small studies do not have the grandeur and the elegance of large, theoretical, highbrow studies that appear to solve all problems except the specific one that evoked the study in the first place. Advertising men, in and out of research, want to fly before they can walk.

The irrationality of the marketplace and the lack of ability to specify what is good or bad advertising constitute a major source of job insecurity for the advertising man. If sales are up, it can be claimed (by the client) that they should be even higher. If sales are down, it can be claimed (by the agency) that only the advertising kept them from going even lower. Since no one "really knows," skill at persuasion, at use of pressure tactics, at politics, and at "human relations" becomes as important in gaining and keeping an account as the "objective reality."

The organizational and personnel problem this presents is decisive. Since the client is the source of all benefits to the agency and its personnel, and since agency personnel are usually better paid than officials in corresponding positions in the client firm, the burden of proof of the agency's efficiency is placed on the agency.

It is unusual when client personnel do not resent the "excessive salaries," the glamorous expense account, and the claims of infallibility that agencies make in their initial solicitation for an account. Their resentment is expressed in excessive demands upon the agency. Tight deadlines, impossible work loads, and unreasonable tasks are presented to the agency as a matter of course. This is often expressed in the phenomenon of the "exercise." The client will present a real or hypothetical marketing or advertising problem to the agency. A short deadline is given, and the implicit or explicit threat is made that retention of the account is based on a satisfactory solution to the problem. The agency personnel are then compelled to work day and night, weekday and weekend, under fantastic costs of money, time, and energy to prove the agency worthy of keeping the account. After all the work is done and the agency has demonstrated its loyalty by dancing to the client's tune, the final report is frequently left unread for weeks or filed away without ever having been read. The agency has, for the time being, paid for the commissions it earns from the largesse of the lower-paid client. In rare instances agencies will resign accounts because of physical or mental breakdowns of key personnel (lower-ranking personnel count less) or because the excessive demands by one client prevent their giving full attention to other, more profitable or less demanding accounts.

The philosophy of the exercise and the attitudes it engenders in agency management are major determinants of relationships within the agency. This is precisely so because the anxiety, powerlessness, and pressure placed upon the agency and its personnel by clients are linked to the extremes of success and failure that are possible because of labor-intensity, the claims for infallibility, and the inability to measure successful advertising.

THE OCCUPATIONAL AND SKILL STRUCTURE OF THE AGENCY

The agency, to repeat, is a service industry that provides intangible skills and counsel to a manufacturing or marketing company. Its product, advertising, is not a standardized product that is mass-produced and sold at low cost to a large number of widely distributed consumers. On the contrary, the final product of the agency—a radio or TV commercial, a print advertisement or a billboard—is made in somewhat the same way as any other piece of art. The difference between genuine art and advertising (as production and not as aesthetics) is that advertising art involves committee planning, consultation, strategy, research, and the coordination of a wide variety of artistic and nonartistic specialists. The former include writers, audio technicians, painters and graphic men, photographers, engravers, cameramen (cinematic or still), musicians, animators, film editors, TV directors, stage designers, and producers. Art in advertising thus may resemble art in architecture or art under a patronage system in which the patron and his minions determine a great deal of the content and execution of the final art product.

Perhaps the only routine and semiautomatic work in advertising is in typing, billing, and clerical work. Production work in the sense of semiskilled or unskilled factory work is almost entirely absent. As estimated earlier, almost 40 percent of total agency personnel are engaged in creative, administrative, professional, or high-level staff work. While it is true that there is a wide variety of higher skills assembled in one relatively small enterprise (600 to 700 people), it is additionally true that the number of people who professionally exercise any one skill is relatively small.

The account supervisor is a man whose major responsibility is to represent the agency to the client, to receive instructions from the client, to make agency recommendations to the client, to coordinate the efforts of the agency in preparing plans and advertising for the client. The account supervisor is in charge of overall supervision of the account, and is concerned with policy, while the account executive is placed in charge of administering the internal operation of the agency as it relates to a particular client.

Working for and with the account supervisor and executive is the account group. The account group consists of creative, technical, and staff specialists, media planners and buyers, researchers, merchandisers and sales-promotion men. Each account group thus is a miniature advertising agency that has a full range of specialists attached to it and is capable of rendering a complete servicing of the account. There are as many account groups in an agency as there are accounts. When the account is a large one, the staff assigned to that account may be employed exclusively on the account in question. When the account is a small one, members of an account group may divide their time between a number of accounts.

Thus the agency usually has a double organization. One set of "bosses" consists of the account supervisor and executive. The other set consists of the heads of individual departments, that is, research director, copy chief or creative director, media director, art director, and so on. Each set of "bosses" has the same employees, and each set has at times different vested interests in the distribution of its employees' time and efforts. The overall agency officers—the president and chairman of the board—are the referees when conflicts occur, and the board of directors offers the formal representation of the various vested interests of both types. Their meetings are the official stage where conflicts are acted out and, if possible, resolved.

Typical conflicts are as follows:

1. When account personnel work on more than one account, their account supervisors may feel that the "part-time" help are spending too much time on other accounts. The account supervisors almost always feel that their account is understaffed. In terms of pressures on the account supervisor, this is probably true.

2. The "part-time" staff usually feel that account supervisors are too demanding. Instead of having two, three, or four part-time jobs, they feel they have that many full-time jobs.

3. The account supervisors quite often feel, especially if their account is not a huge or major one, that the creative and technical staff assigned to them are the rejects, misfits, and incompetents who have been assigned to their account on the basis of lack of ability.

4. Most service personnel are technicians, artists, or specialists, while the account supervisor is either a "business administrator," with no specialized, creative knowledge, or an ex-specialist. As a result, the creative or technical specialist feels that nincompoops, politicians, and incompetents meddle unnecessarily in business they know nothing about. They tend to feel that incompetents among their own bosses and at the client's shop force them to do countless revisions of perfectly good work, or even force them to execute ideas that are so badly conceived or undefined that perfect execution only makes apparent the stupidity of the plans. Thus they feel that most of the work done is totally unnecessary.

5. The account supervisors, on the other hand, feel that the technical specialists are "purists," academicians—tem-

peramental, obstreperous, and difficult. Moreover, they resent the feeling that the technical and creative specialists communicate of being superior and of treating the account executive as if he were a dope.

6. Department heads resent the account heads, frequently feeling that the latter make excessive demands for their accounts on department personnel. They tend to feel that account heads want to tell the service heads and personnel how to do the work that the latter are especially qualified for. They also feel that account heads, to save their own necks, will risk the necks of the service personnel by forcing them to do inferior, dishonest, or unnecessary work. They feel they are obliged to be cat's-paws, rescuing the chestnuts from the fire caused by the negligence and incompetence of account heads.

7. The account heads reciprocate this feeling, justifying their attitudes in terms of the jealousy and intransigence of the heads of the service departments.

8. All the above conflicts are expressed quite often in private gossip, in conflicts over salaries and over the amount and availability of agency stock. The account executive feels that he is the businessman whose job it is to deal with the client, keep him happy, and keep the account in the shop. He has to have tact, to lie, flatter, drink, eat, and live with stupid people in order to keep an account. He must do this by being self-effacing, polite, and deferential even under the pressures of the conscious and unconscious needling and resentment of the client. This entitles him to a lion's share of the rewards.

The technical or creative specialist feels that he does the actual job of planning, creating, and executing the final product (the advertisement) and/or its placement in a medium. Since this is the manifest job of the agency, the lion's share of the reward should be his.

9. In addition, each specialist group develops a special

theory of advertising that just happens to make its function supreme. Copywriters insist that the slogan or apt phrase, the play on words, is the particular ingredient that sells a product. Art directors will stress the symbol and the mood as being especially creative of positive brand images that lead to sales. When images become passé, art directors may insist upon humorous animation. ("You can get across unprovable claims by exaggerating them so much that even if the viewer consciously disbelieves them, he unconsciously accepts them.")

Television producers sell "realistic" and "atmospheric" mood photography, montage effects, use of succession of still shots of puppets to produce "animation"—all techniques designed to transport the viewer out of his normal, hard-headed buying attitude into a world that, because of the suspension of belief, is more "real" than the real world, and within which buying the advertised brand is linked to the fulfillment of the viewer's idealized self-image. Thus the TV producer, too, can make a claim for greater salary and more stock on the basis of attainment of this ideal.

The research director knows no limits to his megalomania except those that he encounters in the resistances that all other departments offer to the inquisitive snooping of research. Research enables the research director to "know" the audience, the customer, the sales personnel, and to "know" the action that will lead to success. He can research everybody's area of competence except his own, and can thus tell everyone else how to do his work. Every other department is forced, in the face of the self-aggrandizing research director, either to limit the operations of research or to control them to serve the special purposes of that department.

Research *does*, however, sometimes provide answers to specific questions, *does* provide an aura of knowing for the agency as a whole, is useful to specialists in providing them with viable alternatives, and is helpful to the account super-

visor in keeping an account and to top management in acquiring accounts. This utility constitutes the claim of the
research director and his department for higher salaries and
a greater share of profits.

10. The assignment of technical and creative specialists
to distinct and separate account groups has additional consequences. While all copywriters, for example, are members
of the creative department, each copywriter actually works
with only a few other copywriters on an account or group
of accounts. He does not work with copywriters other than
those assigned to his own account, though his office will be
in the creative department, next to the offices of all other
copywriters.

His working partners, aside from the few other copywriters on his team, are account heads, artists, television
producers, media planners and buyers, researchers, and so
on. Thus each specialist works primarily with other specialists who have different specialties from his own. Each is competent to judge only his own specialty, and each is required
by the working relationship to make judgments about work
he is not especially qualified to judge.

Since each has the vested interest of his craft, the trained
incompetence or occupational psychosis that characterizes
almost all specialists, each attempts if he can to impose his
own perspective on his account group. But each specialist
has some vested interests in his account group, as opposed to
that of his service departmental peers. The value of his
services is measured by the way his account group has served
to attract and maintain clients. His claim for salary increase
and stock benefits is in part related to the success of his account group. Thus each specialist at times competes against
his occupational peers and his service department.

The pattern of using small numbers of occupational
specialists on an account group, together with other types of
occupational specialists, tends to isolate each from his peers,

to turn specialists into rivals, and to cause them to compete with one another for greater income. Thus the fractionization of the agency into occupational specialties tends to be supplemented by a fractionization of each occupational specialty into account specialties. The individual specialist is thus almost always placed in a cross-pressure between specialty and account. In the short run, he might find it profitable to align himself with his account group. If he does this too obviously or too defiantly, he may risk incurring the enmity of his service department head or of his occupational peers. Thus each service department head would like to insist on the integrity and loyalty of his department in the face of continuous undermining by account supervision.

The competition within a service department is best illustrated by the "creative" competition when a new account enters a shop or when the client requests a new campaign ("the old one is tired"). A number of creative groups (copywriters and artists) are asked to prepare a series of alternative campaigns. Each group is briefed in the background to the account, its past history, its overall marketing, sales, and advertising strategy, and the relevant research background. Each group is given a deadline, and each group prepares prototype advertisements in semifinished form that embody its creative effort. When the deadline has passed, the prototype advertisements are judged by the account supervisors, top agency management, and by the client. The creative group that submits the campaign closest to the one finally adopted usually is assigned to the account. Losers, especially if they were previously assigned to the account in question, are relegated to less important accounts. If one gets the new account assignment, one has a further claim to income and prestige; if one loses too many competitions, one becomes a drifter and is sooner or later forced to find another job.

In such competitions, therefore, the tension is deadly.

Each creative group attempts to keep its major slogan, theme, or strategy a secret, and some groups attempt to ferret out the secrets of other groups in order to steal them, modify them, or develop, by implication only, a neutralizing theme or antidote. Each creative group attempts to "lobby" for its campaign, even though the campaign may exist only as a glimmer in a copywriter's eye; and each may attempt to influence any department that is to evaluate or judge the competition. All relevant parties are drawn into the competition, and each is used as a tool, if it is heedless, of the aspirations of the competing creative groups.

This competition is only an extreme illustration of the normal competition between occupational peers. To some extent such normal competition exists within all departments, and each department member is thus isolated from his peers. To be sure, temporary alliances do exist, based upon common assignments in the present or upon the prospects of profitable assignments in the future. But each man knows that his organizational position can change overnight, that his friends can become his enemies, and vice versa. Thus to walk carefully and watchfully is a *sine qua non* of handling oneself.

11. Since all departments have their sets of rival theories and claims for functional indispensability, the adjudication of such claims is the central function of generalized management.

Advertising agencies organize, disorganize, and reorganize constantly in order to solve the problem of control. In some agencies account supervision is dominant; in others, service departments have major responsibility; and in still others, one department may be supreme. In the latter case, the agency may be known as a "research agency," an "artwork agency," a "copy agency," specializing in either "hardsell" or mood commercials. Other agencies, usually the colossi, sell "total advertising," or total marketing, a claim for excellence in all departments and in all services.

A second function of agency management is to control the account groups. If the account supervisor becomes too strong and has complete control of the client's affections and billings, he can either "blackjack" the agency or walk off with the account. The agency president, board chairman, and service departments are thus forced to develop independent channels of communication to the client that limit the influence of the account supervisor.

SKILL REQUIREMENTS FOR AGENCY PERSONNEL

Artists, copywriters, designers, and other creative personnel to be successful in agency work need to be talented, trained in the exercise of their skill and, if possible, creative. Talent and training are attributes that can be judged (if not measured) by qualified experts, if these are available. Creativity in advertising can be judged only under pressure, if it can be judged at all.

A talented copywriter, without ideas, can go far if he is able to develop the necessary appearances of creativity. Thus when the "Be sociable, have a Pepsi" idea made Pepsi-Cola a major competitor to Coca-Cola, hundreds of brands in all product classes launched advertising that pictured the consumers of these brands as young, modern, carefree, sophisticated, fun-loving, sociable, prosperous, upper-middle-class suburbanites. This image became in a short time a cliché but a highly successful cliché—successful in raising the unspoken wishes of millions of Americans into a self-conscious "model for the millions." The cliché had such wide distribution and penetration that those copywriters and agencies who indiscriminately copied it were not able to establish any distinguishing characteristics for the brands they advertised.

To copy early in the copying cycle may be profitable; to copy late is suicidal. To copy a campaign that is so old that everybody has forgotten it may be a stroke of near genius.

To create a genuine concept, a totally new idea that works, requires as much creativity in advertising as it does in other fields of art, letters, and sciences. Unfortunately, the collective character of the creative enterprise in advertising, and the speed at which both good and bad ideas are copied, make it almost impossible to recognize the original creator.

It is relatively easy to judge the skills of technicians in research, in film editing, in audio departments, in camera work, because there are established techniques in these fields. But even in technical fields the mechanical application of technique results in dull, plodding work. Insight, imagination, the ability to apply technique to the solution of a "business" or aesthetic problem require, even in advertising, the same kinds of artistry that are required of creative personnel. And in these aspects of the work, the criteria for judging a man's work become just as subjective as those used for judging the creative artist.

Media planners, time and space buyers, and buyers of television programs usually develop a great deal of detailed knowledge of their respective fields merely by working in them. No special training is required of the neophyte to enter the field. But once he is in such a field, special talents for detail work, administration, and ability to exercise "good business judgment" are qualities that bring a good man to the fore.

These nontechnical, business and administrative requirements resemble those appropriate to the account. The personnel account executive and supervisor are required to be "good businessmen," good administrators, and to have "good business judgment." In addition, the account administrators are required to be tactful, likable, charming, and to have, to a very high degree, all the qualities of successful salesmen. The similarity in the personal qualities required of the media buyer and the account man frequently results in the promotion of the time and space buyer to account executive, thence to account supervisor, and finally to agency president.

This career pattern is not fixed. Creative personnel, research men, media men, and a wide variety of other occupational types can become account executives; and all types can become agency presidents. But if a specialist is to become an account supervisor or an agency president, he must first exhibit the qualities of the general administrator, businessman, and man of judgment. He has the opportunity to develop these qualities as a department head and administrator, as a member of the board of directors, or in making an impression on important representatives of the client in agency-client meetings or at lunch and after-hours meetings.

Yet a description of the above qualities does not come near to setting forth all the qualities necessary to success in occupational mobility. As indicated above, talent and technical knowledge are desirable qualities for creative and technical personnel. But possession of such qualities results only in the acquisition of rank and position as a staff official. Administrative skill, judgment, and business sense are the terms used to describe the special talents of the nonspecialized businessmen of the agency, who include media and program buyers, account executives and supervisors, and general agency officials. Such lists of qualifications, however, represent only the *public* side of an occupational description. Other, more personal qualities are necessary to complete the description.

Nerve is a central quality that any agency man must possess in order to survive the pressures. Since much of agency work is done under the constant pressure of volume, deadlines, possible criticism, and the ever-present image of total failure, men who cannot "stand the grind" are quickly recognized. Those who can are selected as "comers" and are pushed along as long as they can keep the respect of those who do the pushing.

Nerve means more than the failure to crack under pressure. It means the capacity to exhibit, regardless of the pressures placed on one, calmness, tact, proper deference, good humor, and loyalty to the right people. But these latter qualities are independent of nerve. The ability to exhibit calmness, tact, deference, good humor, and loyalty to the right people is considered to be a basic personality requirement for any account officer, agency officer, or any creative or technical specialist who wants to move upward. For these qualities are client-pleasing qualities. They are also boss-pleasing qualities. Being in a business where one's very existence depends on the "favors" bestowed on one by the client gives advertising a court-like atmosphere. The chief officer of the client is the "king," and the agency personnel are only one set of his courtiers. But the courtiers on each level, by virtue of their acceptance by the throne and by individuals who have access to the throne, receive deference in relationship to their imputed proximity to the throne. Ability to be successful as a courtier becomes objectified, is treated as a psychological trait in and of itself, and becomes the basis for further success in courtsmanship.

The quality of likability (other-orientedness with a purpose) is subject to limitations. In a business where costs are a factor, where pressures are greater than one can absorb by oneself, the ability to resist pressures which are destructive to the individual is a necessary trait for success and for survival. For instance, a client may make demands that are too expensive, too time-consuming, or are impossible of fulfillment. The account executive in this case must either talk the client into modifying his demands or convince him that his demands have been fulfilled when they have not. At times he may be able to convince the client that the demands are totally unreasonable. But whatever he does, the account executive must do so in a manner that gains the respect or the liking of the client. If the account executive gives in to such demands, he may embarrass the agency and its profit structure, overload the technical, administrative, and creative staffs who have to meet the demands, and find himself in trouble with his own office. Moreover, if the account executive indicates to the client that he can be pushed around, he invites the resentful or sadistic client to do just that. Finally, some clients expect top agency personnel to have convictions, policies, and beliefs of their own. They are paid to have these attributes. The account executive who is so likable that he accedes to whatever the client wishes is simply not doing his job. He is not providing the client with the counsel which is part of the service of the agency. If he does disagree, however, he must be tactful and, above all, he must know when to stop disagreeing. This *realistic toughness* is the third major quality necessary for success in an agency.

The three major personality traits so far discussed become the basis for types of agency personnel. The types are as follows:

Type 1. The Creative Genius.   This is the official who creates or attempts to create the impression that his technical knowledge or creative ability is so great that he can ignore the other realities of the agency business. If he succeeds (by being almost as good as he claims to be), he can go far toward a top staff position. He is usually viewed as irresponsible in positions that require "judgment" or administrative ability.

Type 2. The Likable Chap.   He works hard and is continually on the run. He is pleasing, amiable, entertaining, and quite frequently provides more services than the client or account supervisor asks for. He is perfectly eager and willing to handle all details for his superiors, or to get someone else to do so. But he is at a total loss when two or more superiors disagree, or when he is asked to have an opinion before an official opinion exists. He lacks nerve. Such a person is not likely to reach a position higher than account executive because he finds it difficult to work without lines and because he is likely to give away his own, his subordinates' and, worse, the agency's shirt in the desire to please. He needs to work under Type 3.

Type 3. The Tough Realist. He may not have creative or technical ability but knows how to please when that quality is necessary. He knows when to get tough with his subordinates, with himself ("discipline"), and with the client. He knows in any given situation what his self-interest is, what the client's interests are, and what the agency's, account group's, or service department's interests are. No matter what the social situation is, he knows how to juggle these interests so that he, in the final analysis, will come out on top. Of course, such results do not always occur. When two or more tough realists come into open conflict, one may be forced to go (even if this means his occupational demise). One can make an error in judgment, such as cultivating and supporting an important official in the client firm, only to discover later that this "personal" client has been squeezed out. The enemies of the personal client may now be running the client firm, and the agency man is *persona non grata*. If this happens, the tough realist may be out of a job. A tough realist may spend a decade cultivating a particular individual in the client firm, nursing him up the ladder of success in his own firm. Shortly after the client "arrives," he dies. The tough realist then loses his "contact" and may have no other assets of value when he faces his own agency.

The three types can be conceived of as polar types. Most personnel in an agency, however, exhibit combinations of the traits of the three polar types. The creative genius can also be a likable chap or a tough realist (if he is willing to suppress his needs for personal recognition) but he cannot be both. The likable chap is likely to be a pure type. However, a likable account executive, after achieving that position, may suddenly begin to sound like a tough realist. If he can maintain that attitude under pressure or adversity, he may grow up to be a genuine tough realist. The tough realist may have had, in the earlier years of his career, creative or technical ability which, by and large, he is not able to exercise in the present because of the pressures of other work. He can always be likable when necessary. But the quality that accounts for his success is his realistic toughness.

THE "MEANING OF WORK" IN AN ADVERTISING AGENCY

Our discussion of the economic, occupational, social, and psychological structure of the advertising agency defines much of what can be said of the "meaning of work" in an agency. For the very framework and operation of the agency constitute a set of limitations and opportunities for the individual. What these limitations and opportunities are to a particular individual is a function of the nature of the social structure within which he works, his particular needs, motivation, and personality, and the particular way his personality is linked to that social structure.

The phrase "meaning of work" is an ambiguous term. "Meaning" can be conceived of as the immanent set of meanings that attach to an *objective* event, situation, or social structure. In this sense work can be conceived of as being meaningful in and of itself, without the support of external rewards and gratifications which are a product of the work but are not in the work. This immanent meaning can be contrasted to instrumental meanings in which the "meaning" (the satisfaction one gets from the work) is not in the work itself but in what the work enables one to do in other areas of life. Thus dull routine or painful work, work that contains no joy, can be meaningful if, by doing it, one achieves an economic gain, prestige, power, or even the perfection of a skill that is useful for the attainment of some other goal. With these distinctions in mind we can pose the question: What are the internal and external meanings attached to work in an advertising agency?

It is simplest to discuss external meaning. As we have previously indicated, advertising work is extremely well paid, has tremendous opportunities for mobility, and in a high-tax economy offers a capable man great opportunities to acquire wealth. Such economic motivations need not necessarily imply that the advertising man is a crass materialist. The acquisition of wealth, in a society that is heir to the Protestant ethic, is simply a means for a man to legitimate himself in terms of the only standards that may be meaningful to him. Certainly economic and social mobility through success in advertising may mean to an individual that he is on his way to fulfilling the American dream. His efforts, his manhood, his ideals are affirmed by his success. The successful man can hold his head up high in his community and can gain the respect of his wife, friends, and neighbors if they happen to share his dream. He develops confidence, poise, assertiveness, and even arrogance in his relationships with others outside the industry, no matter how timid and "likable" he is in the agency. Moreover, the upwardly mobile agency man earns almost sufficient income to acquire a life-style that conforms to his image of what middle- and upper-class life is like. He can play at being a solid citizen, an upper bohemian, or an English-type country squire. Each type of play is a further affirmation of his version of the American dream, and therefore must be taken seriously. But mobile advertising men are usually intelligent, articulate, educated, and expert at seeing through false appearances, including their own. They have this ironic talent because they are marginal men and because their occupational selection and function require them to construct "artificial worlds" which can enchant and seduce outsiders. This talent for analysis cannot be "turned off" when it comes to the analysis of oneself. Thus in playing the solid citizen, the upper bohemian, or the English country squire, advertising men tend to burlesque themselves, doing so half with tongue in cheek and half seriously. This comic aspect of one's private life is frequently presented to friends in the profession, but a more serious demeanor is presented to outsiders.

The thousands of jokes about advertising men, the satires of the language of advertising ("Let's put it [an idea] on at New Haven and see where it gets off" or "Let's get down on our hands and knees and look at it from the client's point of view") are inventions of successful advertising men who cannot genuinely understand their own success because that success appears to be based on so little. Self-deprecation is one of the prices one pays for what is thought of as unearned success.

Part of this ironical attitude, which is based on the notion of "pinch me—it may not be so," derives from the fact that it may not be "so" tomorrow. For the mobile advertising man realizes, perhaps not openly, that a single job failure at the age of forty-five or over by a man with a salary of $20,000 and over may make it all "not so." Thus he can never accept fully, at all levels of his consciousness, the success he might otherwise believe in. To outsiders he may act the role of the successful executive. To the few insiders whom he feels he does not have to "sell," he may confide his anxieties or ironies. The anxieties emerge in pressure-cooker situations, and the ironies in success situations.

An additional set of supporting external meanings is found in the idea that the advertising man makes important decisions for big companies, representing hundreds of millions of dollars of annual sales or billions of dollars of corporate wealth. The young advertising executive, and even an older one, may confide to his wife or friend that he sat in a meeting with the president of a giant corporation and perhaps even said something. He may point to a commercial that is on the air, and say: "See that commercial? I wrote one line of it!" or he may say in irony, "I recommended against it." He can speak knowingly about the inner affairs of gigantic American corporations to his male friends, or speak even more knowingly about soaps, detergents, floor polishes, foods, and sauces to his wife and his wife's friends. When "the business of America is business," being close to business and to the thrones of the monarchs of business is enchanting.

To the successful advertising man who is himself the son of a successful father, success in advertising has different meanings. Success means the validation of one's birthright, the proof that one has lived up to the task handed down by one's father or family. Success, then, is both a right and a duty; failure is a disgrace. The upper-class advertising man is less likely to develop the ironic self-mockery of the upwardly mobile man. He is likely to take the surrealistic atmosphere of advertising seriously, to accept its rituals, and act unselfconsciously. He is likely to be reliable in dealing with clients because he does not let the mask slip; he has no mask. Therefore he is capable of genuine sincerity in an industry where sincerity is a major stock-in-trade. The sincere upper-class advertising man is not likely to understand the ironic, sardonic, and self-deprecating mobile man. He feels that such a man will befoul his own nest, will risk upsetting the client, and will regard him as being "thick" or stupid.

These mutual feelings of lack of admiration, however, are usually not expressed; they are kept behind the façades of deference and authority that reflect the respective positions of the individuals in question. Occasionally they are expressed directly; more often they are expressed between two individuals of similar class and occupational position.

Most often they result in the fact that individuals of diverse backgrounds do not understand each other.

A third external meaning of advertising work comes from the enjoyment of the glamour of advertising. This includes enjoyment of the food and drink in fancy restaurants, the enjoyment being more a function of the expense than the quality of the food, the drink, or the company. The idea of air travel, with sudden and long trips for short conferences, stays at expensive hotels, and living on the expense account all make life exciting when discussed with outsiders or with the less fortunate. One quickly becomes an authority on exotic foods, restaurants, hotels, and cities, and can compare notes with the equally fortunate. The glamour of advertising supports the feeling of success that mobility may bring, and it sometimes provides a substitute for more tangible success. Most pathetically, one frequently hears of newly graduated college students who, in applying for an advertising job, cite as their reason the glamour of the job, as well as the economic opportunities or the chance to come close to what they regard as the sources of power and the throne.

Another form of external meaning can come from acceptance of the public ideology. Hypothetically, this meaning pattern would be stated as follows: "Advertising is a service not to me personally or to the clients only, but to the economy as a whole. It keeps the economy going, creates new products, new jobs, makes industry competitive, and helps to bestow the advantages of free enterprise on our economy." This ideology is the basis for the theme and rhetoric of after-dinner speeches, interviews with and articles by distinguished leaders of the advertising industry, advertising and marketing professors, and industrialists speaking or writing for public consumption.

We have described this service ideology as a hypothetical system of meaning. It is hypothetical because it represents a possibility but not an actuality. Advertising men simply do not speak in these terms in personal conversation. At most, a top official will utter such sounds in an informal group when he is practicing for a speech or writing a paper for public consumption. If he does this among his peers, they are likely to interject wry comments. They may well document his speech with examples of conspicuous waste, stupidity, or mismanagement, conducted either by advertising men or by their clients. Even upper-class top officials who take advertising seriously are not likely to indulge in "speechmaking" in intimate circles, if only to avoid such wry comment.

On the contrary, most advertising men compile and treasure the conspicuous boners, the waste and fatuousness that advertisers and their agencies commit. Stories are circulated about the most sensational television buy of the decade, bought by a company that was so late in reaching a buying decision that it had to buy the only show available, against its inclinations—a show that all other companies and agencies who had been offered it had turned down. Other such stories concern the successful man who moves upward and onward by ruining everything he touches; the company that researches a product so long and so well that, by the time it is done with its research, its competitors have preempted the market; the company whose advertising and marketing policies and operations can be turned into a casebook on how not to advertise or market a brand. Advertising men sometimes discuss the Cold War with the hope that the Russians have a number of marketing and advertising men in their top ranks to balance the odds a little. It is hoped that the Russians can foul up at least as often as American industry.

Ideology, as it is publicly expressed, then, does not provide meaning in the sense that such meaning may sustain the motivations of individuals. At best it provides a claim for the respectability and legitimacy of the industry, a claim made by individuals who do not believe the claim in any operative sense. Very few advertising men will, however, deny the ideology of advertising in public. To do so would rock the boat, result in a public squabble, and invite clients to withdraw their advertising from agencies that employ controversial characters.

The operative external meanings of work can be conceived of as those surrounding economic gain, and the glamour and self-importance achieved by working in an important industry, and not by an ideology of service.

INTERNAL MEANINGS IN ADVERTISING

As previously indicated, internal meanings derive from joy in performing an activity for the sake of the activity itself, and not for the external products of that activity. At first glance, this category of meaning appears to be most applicable to creative personnel and to technologists. The writer, the artist, the designer, the musical composer, the trained researcher—all enter the agency with specialized interests, talents, and training in their respective fields. Working in advertising gives the artist or technologist an opportunity to be paid for exercising his creative ability, his craft, or his specialized methodology on "real, live problems" where his art and science can have some effect.

If this is the hope that brings a talented individual into advertising, he is doomed to quick disappointment. For the creative artist or technologist discovers almost immediately that advertising writing, art, and science are not for the small magazine, the gallery, or the scientific journal (except marketing journals). The problems he works on are selected by others. The strategy he works on is the product of countless, boring meetings with artistic or scientific nincompoops. At each stage of his work, the Philistines make suggestions, and interfere. When a work is done, the Philistines reject the already compromised mess because it does not meet the specifications they were unaware of when they commissioned the work. So back he goes to the drawing board to start all over again under much the same conditions.

The creative man or technologist begins to arrive at a genuine understanding of advertising when he realizes that his work is a tool, a means of achieving goals that lie outside the work itself. Such goals consist of getting the job done on time in a manner that is satisfactory to someone else (if not to his former self), of helping his boss, his department, his agency, and his client to do the job they were assigned, and of getting properly rewarded for successful completion of his work. All these meanings may be admirable, but frequently they are meanings that an individual discovers after he has been in advertising for some time, and after he has been disappointed or broken in the attempt to do what he regards as more creative, scientific, or serious work.

Individuals who enter advertising with less grandiose aspirations are less likely to be disenchanted, but they are also less likely to do creative work in advertising. This is because even burned-out ideals and creativity, when not accompanied by bitterness, allow the creative or scientific technician to approach the creation of an advertisement with some of the talent, sensitivity, and techniques that a dedicated artist and scientist can bring to noncommercial work.

Thus the exposure to agency work tends to turn internal meanings into external meanings. Work tends to lose its meaning-for-itself and to develop instrumental meanings.

There are, of course, limitations to this process. A major limitation consists in the persistence of the instinct for workmanship, pride in craftsmanship, in doing a sound, workmanlike job. Pride in craftsmanship appears to be as central to the personality of a creative individual as any other trait. It is the last quality to disappear. Thus most creative and scientific personnel will continue to strive for technical ex-

cellence in their work regardless of whether they think the
work they are asked to do is badly conceived, is inartistic
or unscientific, or essentially is not their own. More conflicts
between creative and noncreative personnel take place over
techniques than over aesthetics or over ethics. This is because technical virtuosity is the last remnant of a man's
pride in his creative ability. To the layman or to a specialist
in another field, it is a source of considerable amusement,
and at times ennui, to see two creative specialists or technicians fighting tooth and nail (but politely) over minor
points of technique that do not appear to affect the strategy,
overall design, or imputed results of an advertisement. However, such concern for detail usually results in technically
accomplished advertising.

For the noncreative, nontechnical person in advertising
there should, at first appearance, be no internal meaning to
his work. His job is primarily administrative in nature. It
involves keeping track of the flow of paper through channels,
and accelerating, stopping, or restarting that flow. It involves
"selling" to superiors and clients, and manipulating, planning, coaxing, and coercing cooperation and work out of
inferiors and peers. He comes to such tasks with no particular interest, talent, or creative genius. By and large, his
motivations for getting into the field are: it pays well, it
sounds glamorous and exciting, and there is nothing else he
really wants to do. Once he becomes an advertising man, he
really discovers all the opportunities for advancement, the
excitement and the glamour and the possibilities for failure,
the pressures, the overwork, the conspiracies, the powerlessness, the isolation, and the anxiety that are recurrent in the
course of his career.

Gentle personalities are likely to get out of advertising at
relatively young ages. If they are "businessmen," they will
try to move to large corporations where, at lower levels and
at lower pay, the pressures and crises are less frequent and

less turbulent. If they have merchandisable talents, they may try teaching, government, or some other stable field. This process of interindustry mobility results in a shakedown, leaving as survivors those who think they have nerve, toughness, talent, or other personal qualities necessary for the life of a courtier. Those who discover that they do not have these qualities, or do not have enough of them to maintain a career after they are well started on that career, are the genuine tragedies in advertising. They may be too successful to get out, but not strong enough to stay in. Individuals in this situation are the ones who break under pressure.

But to the strong, the nervy, the talented and tough, the very fact of pressure constitutes the strongest set of internal meanings possible. For the difficulties, the pressure, the politics and manipulation, the irrationality, the powerlessness and the isolation all constitute a challenge to one's manhood. The challenge is "be crushed or survive." The answer the advertising man gives is: "Throw everything you can at me —work, pressure, senselessness—and somehow I will lick you and force you to throw even more work at me. Each victory will make me more able to survive new challenges, since my nerve and toughness will be greater and my skills will have been tested in more encounters." The response is a Promethean challenge to the gods and the fates.

The satisfaction involved is a sense of delight in knowing that one has succeeded in manipulating others, of "selling" the bosses or the client, defying the gods and the fates. If nerve and realistic toughness are the supremely valued traits of the tough realist, then awareness of one's exhibition and possession of these traits becomes a value in and of itself. Income, stock ownership, even the glamour of advertising and the way of life deriving from advertising, are merely external affirmations of an inner attitude. The inner attitude, not the results, are the chief value that excites the driving, tough businessman.

In a literary or philosophical imagery this meaning pattern can be called "Faustian." The Faustian man seeks goals outside himself that are difficult. His inner goals are to master the difficult, not to possess the goal, and to exercise his strength and talent in overcoming the obstacles. It is the feeling of strength, confidence, pride in mastery, and the recognition he gets from others for his ability that constitute the source of his joy in work.

In psychological terms, this meaning pattern can be called narcissism. It is an intensified form of self-love because the satisfactions derived from activity are a self-conscious pride in achievement. The narcissistic individual, even in the midst of the most difficult work and pressure, keeps an area of his consciousness detached from his work. He becomes his own observer, checking on himself and commenting on his performance, as he manipulates himself and others. He works in a frenzy, and praises or condemns himself as he does so. In the sense that the detached observer in him robs him of the capacity to feel anything spontaneously, none of his feelings are "genuine." Even if he acts or speaks spontaneously, the narcissistic observer does an ironic or detached analytical commentary on the action, saying, "Nicely done, boy," or, "You'll have to do better next time."

The driving ambition of the narcissist, then, is to win the plaudits of his own inner cheering stand. When he does so, the psychological tone he exhibits is euphoria, brazen self-confidence, aggressiveness, and optimism. When he fails, the psychological tone is depression, self-pity, paranoia, and feelings of rejection. But since the narcissist is self-conscious, he knows that if he can generate the attitudes of self-confidence, euphoria, and aggressiveness, he is likely to sound sincere, convincing, and effective.

Thus one of the most humorous and charming situations in advertising occurs when an account supervisor and his minions are about to make a presentation to the client. After all the work has been done, and the presentation, the charts, the film, the reports are all "locked up" and produced, several days are spent in meetings, rehearsals, and conversations during which each member of the team stokes up the enthusiasm and self-confidence of all others. Woe unto the hapless observer who wittingly or unwittingly discovers a flaw in operation, or throws cold water on it. He destroys the self-confidence of the team, their enthusiasm, sincerity, and capacity for doing effective work. Collective narcissism is a necessary ingredient for teamwork.

Narcissism has other advantages for the advertising man. The source of narcissism is the basic energy of the individual. But with narcissism, all the energy is turned inward, and becomes self-love. The individual gives this energy to himself and tells himself to use it in such a way that narcissism can grow and grow and grow. Thus the narcissist in his euphoric stages has immense reserves of energy, confidence, and aggressiveness that he can direct at narcissistic purposes. He can work at top speed under the worst of pressure for extended periods of time until he collapses either from failure or from physical and psychological fatigue. The demands, the pressures, that advertising work places on the advertising man, then, are appropriate to the narcissist.

However, the narcissistic energy evoked by the man and his job cannot be shut off at will. The energy once released needs an outlet, and will rattle and shake its owner if there is no outlet. In advertising, the flow of work is uneven; in between crises, storms, and drives there are sometimes extended periods of calm. After the individual has recovered his strength from the last crisis, any further period of calm becomes a threat. The restless energy wants to be released. Advertising men solve this problem in a number of ways. Severe measures to bottle up the energy can be taken at the risk of depression. Narcissistic energy can be released in drinking, entertaining, partying, carousing, and active and demanding vocations and sports. All these are parts of the way of life of many advertising men. Finally, if there is no crisis, one can always be provoked. This can be done consciously, by starting a new round of solicitations for new business; or it can be done unconsciously by starting a fight with a peer, the client, or another department. One can demand an "exercise" to keep one's subordinates busy; or one can feud and fuss out of lack of interest in routine, calm, peaceful work.

If narcissism is turned into useless burning of unnecessary energy, it becomes self-destructive. The individual wears himself out physically and emotionally, moves from crisis to crisis and from exhaustive breakdown to breakdown. He dies before his time. If he uses his narcissism to provoke crises, feuds, self-dramatizing arguments and quarrels, the narcissist can precipitate crises in others, causing conflict and resentments that can wreck an organization.

Narcissism is a generalized psychological trait that can erupt in anyone. As such, it is not linked particularly to advertising. Narcissism can be linked to any kind of work— it merely means that one is preoccupied with the response to one's self in work rather than with the work itself. Narcissism is likely to be a dominant characteristic in the creative and performing arts where the person releases tremendous energies to act more for an audience consisting of himself than for the audience in the seats. It is likely to be present in politics where the demands on the public personality are so great that only an individual who enjoys his public performance can endure the strain of that performance. It is also likely to be found to a high degree in other industries where the occupational strains and stresses are similar to those of advertising. These include public relations, the mass media, management consulting, and the upper levels of all large-scale organizations.

But it is true that narcissism is found to a very great extent in advertising. Why this should be so can be explained in terms of the structure of advertising. Individuals with

creative talent or with scientific aspirations who are intrinsi-
cally interested in their work are driven out of the industry
if they insist that work be internally meaningful. If they
remain in advertising, it is because their work has become
instrumental to them. To say that work is instrumental is to
say that the work becomes at the same time an object and a
means for the individual. The man is separated from his
work by self-consciousness, narcissism. Advertising thus
makes narcissists out of non-narcissists.

In the same way, the noncreative businessman finds that
tremendous pressures, difficulties, obstacles, and anxieties are
placed in the path of achieving substantial but extrinsically
meaningful rewards. The pressures are so great that those
who cannot take them leave. Those who remain are the ones
who thrive on work and pressure, who enjoy work and pressure for what these enable them to accomplish. Those who
remain are the narcissists.

Thus advertising modifies and selects personalities so that
a few predominant types are produced. To the extent that
advertising has the public image of being glamorous, exciting, close to the source of power, and frenzied, it attracts
individuals who think they might survive in this atmosphere.
Even the negative image of advertising serves as a recruiting
poster to those who find the "negative image" positive. In
this sense advertising recruits potential or actual narcissists
as well as it selects and creates narcissists from those who
unwittingly enter its domain.

PERSONAL ETHICS IN ADVERTISING

Much of our previous discussion frames the discussion of
the role of ethics in advertising. The word "ethics," however, is an ambiguous term. For our present purposes,
"ethics" does *not* include the following:

1. Rules and regulations governing the competition between agencies, involving such "crimes" as account stealing,

speculative unsolicited presentations to secure a new account, and raiding of personnel. We abstain from such discussion because we are concerned with personal ethics rather than with institutional or trade-association policies.

2. For the same reasons we are not concerned with the law, FTC, USDA, and FCC regulations per se. The extent to which individuals regard the law as a barrier to their personal goals is, of course, of some interest.

3. We are not concerned with ethics in an absolute sense, as perhaps expressed by the Golden Rule. The Golden Rule is too severe a standard to judge any industry by, and would not distinguish one industry from another. However, very few people in Western civilization can discuss ethics without having in the "back of the mind" the Judeo-Christian concept of ethics. For our present discussion we shall leave such ethics in the back of the mind, allowing them to emerge when and where they must.

The operational definition of ethics we are forced to use is as follows: Those actions or rules for action which, when violated, produce in the violator, a spectator, or a person informed of the action, a sense of moral shock, disgust, or horror. The reverse of this definition also applies: Ethics are not operative when an "expected sense of horror" does not follow the commission or the knowledge of the action. In short, an action is viewed as ethical when it does not produce a negative judgment on moral grounds. It is viewed as unethical when it does.

ETHICS IN DEALING WITH THE PUBLIC

Since the economic function of advertising is to help a manufacturer sell his brand, the evaluation of ethics might start with a consideration of what advertising men believe is ethical or unethical in the claims, promises, and techniques they use toward this end.

Complaints by Newton Minow and the FTC have revealed to the public that a great deal of "fraudulent" advertising is central to the day-to-day operations of the agency and its clients. Fake demonstrations appear in the commercials; fraudulent claims are made; misleading statements are presented as statistical facts. Product weaknesses are covered over—in fact, made into virtues. Any reading of FTC circulars, newspapers, or the speeches by Newton Minow will reveal that part of the day-to-day fraud that government officials can discover as meeting the legal definitions of fraud.

Our discussion does not hinge on the fact that fraudulent or misleading advertising exists, but on the attitude of agency personnel to commercials that might be construed as fraudulent.

Agency personnel recognize as primary their economic function to help their client sell his brand. Anything that helps is useful, even fraudulent or misleading advertising. This is especially true if the brand has no unusual characteristics to make it attractive to the public. The copywriter or the account executive can paraphrase Winston Churchill, and say, "It is not my duty to preside at the liquidation of my client." This is all the more true if the advertised product is inferior to other brands. For in such cases, the copywriter's pride in craftsmanship is invoked ("Anybody can sell a product that sells itself, but it takes art to sell an inferior product"). Thus if a hairdressing is too greasy, one inverts the weakness by saying, "A little dab will do you . . . or the girls will pursue you." If the major cleaning ingredient in your client's detergent is so ineffective that it requires twice as much of that ingredient to equal the cleaning ability of the major competitor, you claim "twice the active cleaning ingredients." If your brand needs two or more ingredients to do the work that other products do with one ingredient, you advertise "twin-power" or "just like a doctor's prescription." If your product was inferior and a minor change has been made to make it almost equal to its competitors, you advertise it as "new," "improved," or "25 percent better" (better than what is not specified). You might add just enough of a "miracle" ingredient (lanolin, hexachlorophene, olive oil, and so on) to be able to advertise the ingredient but not enough to affect the cost or the product quality. You might even study the manufacturing process and discover a standard ingredient of all brands in the product class which no one has yet advertised, and then proceed, by advertising, to transform this into a new "miracle" ingredient.

You may employ your research department to use technically accurate and honest surveys that lead, because of the glories of an ambiguous English language and grammar, to "dishonest" conclusions: "80 percent of all doctors prescribe the *ingredients* in our brand" (but the vast majority do not recommend the brand—in fact, may recommend against using the brand). Questionnaires are designed so that only one answer is possible, and subsequent research work is scrupulously honest; the results are impeccable, and are used to provide the legal basis for an advertising claim.

At each point in this process, pride in craftsmanship enables the creative man to provide the client with "selling" advertising despite brand deficiencies. Even when one has a brand that is technically superior, but whose superiority is the result of highly technical and difficult-to-understand features, it is frequently more efficient to develop a simple, fraudulent claim or demonstration than to demonstrate the difficult truth.

In all these cases, the primary criteria for advertising honesty is not the honesty or dishonesty of the advertising but its imputed selling efficiency.

So far as one can be certain, advertising men do not object to telling these "necessary" lies. In fact, when the necessary lie is a creative one, they take great pride in their ability to overcome the deficiencies of the product. Some indications of malaise, however, are found in the ironical ways in which they will recount their creative escapades. Ironical pride may indicate that, if they could not tell the truth, they at least did a good job of lying. Thus virtuosity in fraud becomes a virtue. For the most part, however, even the desire to commit fraud is limited to that which is necessary to sell the brand.

Quite frequently advertisers will be more interested in truth-telling than agency people, especially copywriters. First of all, since they are not copywriters, they do not get the aesthetic satisfaction, except vicariously, from producing the creative lie; and second, the client suffers more than an individual copywriter from being the object of an FTC cease-and-desist order. Such an order may be worth millions of dollars of negative advertising for a brand. To avoid such problems, a crew of high-priced agency, client, and media lawyers inspect all copy and certify its probable legality before finished advertisements are prepared. Such precautions are necessary. The creative man, if given full freedom, will at times generate such patently fraudulent advertising that only a lawyer can stop him. Such creativity, however, is relatively infrequent. Most copywriters are aware of the legal limitations and, if they are not sure of them, will consult the lawyers in advance.

Nevertheless, a few copywriters do get the reputation of being moral lepers; they love fraud for fraud's sake. Such individuals will rejoice in the complicated, tricky, aesthetically satisfying lie even when the truth might be a powerful selling proposition. The moral leper is spotted almost as soon as he joins the agency. His fantastic lies (both in copywriting and in personal relations) are told and retold by all others. He is a source of humor to those not directly involved in working with him, and a source of danger and chagrin to all others. He is a source of danger because, in risking legal action, he endangers the account. Moreover, everyone connected with the moral leper (and technically he is a psychopath) must attempt to avoid or repair the harm he does to the agency and to others. He therefore causes more work than he accomplishes. However, a psychopath can be a good copywriter if he is controlled. There are few limits to his fancy, his imagination, or his ability to beg, borrow, or steal ideas that may be useful.

But the moral leper is the deviant that defines the important, operative ethical norms for advertising. He establishes the boundaries that must not be crossed. If one does pass over, one receives moral disapprobation. In relation to the public, this norm can be stated as follows: *"Don't tell an unnecessary lie."* Necessary lies are acceptable because they are essential to fulfill the economic function of the agency. What is more, all advertising men tend to be conscious of the pressures that all other men work under. They are sympathetic to the individual who suffers from moral and ethical lapses in response to these pressures. They are totally unsympathetic to the individual who enjoys lying, or to the person who lies beyond what is structurally necessary. Thus, in a genuine sense, most advertising men are profoundly moral.

ETHICS IN DEALING WITH CLIENTS

The client is the advertising man's sole source of bread and butter. In addition to being well aware of this fact, the advertising man has other images of the client, which include the following:

Most clients are stupid. If they weren't, they'd be working in agencies where they'd get paid more.

Most clients are technically incompetent.

Most clients are sadistic, or resentful of the agency man because of the latter's ability and salary.

Most clients are unreasonable and overdemanding. They also stick their noses into business they are not equipped to handle.

Most clients are hungry, thirsty, and vain. They need constant attention, flattery, and fake deference.

Most clients are ingrates. They will switch accounts for petty reasons, especially after the agency has done a superhuman job.

Most clients want the credit for work well done, and will blame the agency for their own mistakes.

Some clients are gullible fools, but these are nice people.

All the above images are not applied to all clients. In fact, each agency will have one or more clients whose personal qualities, business acumen, and administrative ability set so high a standard that all other clients look feeble in comparison.

These images set the stage for the discussion of client-focused ethics. The fundamental strategy of the agency is to make convincing its claim for distinctive agency superiority and indispensability in meeting the client's needs. Once one acquires the account, the initial argument plus its proof must be continuously demonstrated, even in the face of falling sales ("They could, under other circumstances, fall even faster").

Ethics in relationship to the client are based on the norm *"Don't ever tell a direct lie to the client."* This may not even be an ethical norm, since it is based on the assumption that without the client's trust in one's basic honesty, no enduring client-agency relationship is possible. The norm is thus a pragmatic device to keep the account.

If we consider the rule as an ethical norm, however, another set of normative propositions follow. While one does not tell a lie to the client, one does not always have to tell the total truth. The agency's fundamental business requirement is to keep profitable accounts. Therefore, agency communications to the client tend to conceal negative aspects of agency operations—inefficiency, indecision, or lack of attention to his account because major attention has been given to other accounts. It is assumed that clients are big boys and that it is their problem to discover the negative aspects of the client-agency relationship, not the duty of the agency to inform on itself.

When an account is secure, however, the agency may criticize its own advertising, volunteer research results that are negative, or otherwise criticize its own operation, especially if the agency is immediately prepared to take protective action. Such self-criticism builds trust and forestalls client-originated criticism.

The deviant individuals in client-agency ethics are of two types. The *schlemiel* who reveals agency difficulties to the client (either by accident or as an attempt to curry favor) is a menace who cannot be kept around. The moral leper, on the other hand, who tells the client lies that are too big, risks creating a basic mistrust by allowing himself and the agency to be exposed as "defrauding" the client. He is the worst menace. Between these two extremes are the tough realists who know how and when to tell the truth.

The "tough realist" client is respected but feared because there is less need to manipulate him and less danger of a sudden disenchantment. The tough realist expects more and less of the agency at the same time. He does not ask for miracles, but he does ask for hard, creative work. A good agency can provide this without the necessity for deception.

THE ETHICS OF INTERPERSONAL RELATIONSHIPS

There are a few general norms that apply to all people in an agency, and a great many that apply to specific types of social relationships. The general ones are considered first.

An overall rule is: *"Don't lie, cheat, steal unnecessarily."* This is the same rule as applied to the public, but now applied as a norm for interpersonal relations. Again the same general limits apply. A great many otherwise unacceptable actions are viewed as tolerable (except to the injured party) because all are aware of the pressure that causes individuals to act in ways that are outside the Judeo-Christian ethical framework. The individual whose ethical lapses are due only to a desire for personal advantage or for "joy through crime" is viewed as a moral leper. If one lies to avoid endangering the agency or to avoid losing one's job, then the lie is necessary.

Another norm involves keeping one's promises. The rule is: *"Don't make empty promises; but when you make a promise, keep it."* This is a general application of the norm of not lying to the client. The individual must establish himself as being trustworthy. To do so he must keep his personal promises. However, he should not place himself in embarrassing situations by giving promises he cannot meet. Personal honor, in this sense, is one of the most valued qualities in a man. Word-keeping indicates "character," and helps a man to gain the reputation of being "responsible"—an indispensable quality for mobility to "business-oriented" positions.

The demand for word-keeping is nevertheless not so

stringent as may first appear. If there is a choice between keeping one's word to a client or a superior, and keeping it to a peer or an inferior, the choice is always made in favor of the former. This is excusable if the promise was made in good faith and if the conflict in promises was unavoidable. Again, all parties recognize the pressures involved.

The moral leper makes indiscriminate promises that he has no intention of fulfilling, or which he fails to fulfill simply because of inconvenience.

A third general rule involves one's private life. The agency makes no demands on the individual's private morals, ethics, or character so long as they do not impinge upon the conduct of business or on agency-client relationships. An individual can be a homosexual, a lecher, a drunk, or a psychopath just so long as he is discreet. He should not display his vices in the office, nor should he get his name in the papers. The client, in short, should think of an agency man as a pillar of the community unless, of course, the client is a lecher or a semialcoholic himself. In that case, the agency man may assist the client in assuaging his vicious needs. But in every case, the obligation is to keep one's ill-fame out of the newspapers.

As for their personal standards of judgment, agency men appear to be tolerant of others' idiosyncrasies as long as they are not obtrusive or threatening. One does not impose one's personal taste on others.

A final rule, more a job requirement than an ethical norm, is *"Never lose your temper, no matter what the provocation."* Losing one's temper causes the individual to say things, or expose things, that are best left unsaid. Personal control is a means of avoiding "spilling the beans." And spilling the beans is one of the most serious violations of agency norms. Being a vicious gossip, in or not in anger, is almost automatic grounds for firing.

ETHICS FOR BOSSES WITH RESPECT
TO THEIR SUBORDINATES

A boss is expected to give credit to juniors for work they have done. He should not "hog" the glory. It is assumed that, since most work in an agency is collective work, it is not necessary for one man to have all the credit. Moreover, since the boss recruits, hires, trains, and supervises the work of his subordinates, credit for a subordinate's outstanding work automatically belongs to the boss. Since this is true, the boss gets the credit, even if he graciously renounces it in favor of his subordinates. The boss who "hogs the glory," then, takes the credit he would get anyway, but takes it by denying it unnecessarily to others. He gets the reputation of being a moral leper, and subordinates seek to transfer from his jurisdiction, if necessary to another agency. They may even attempt to keep their ideas secret, announcing them only in public meetings in which their bosses' peers or superiors (including representatives of the client) are present.

Similarly, a boss is expected to take the blame for a subordinate's mistake, even though the boss is not responsible for the mistake. He is viewed as responsible for hiring the miscreant and for supervising his work. If a mistake reaches that point where it can be publicly called a mistake, the boss has failed. If he is a "man," he will take the blame in public and settle with the subordinate in private.

This norm is again limited by the norm of pressure. If the boss is endangered personally by the mistake of the subordinate, it is "understood" when he allows the subordinate to take the blame. If he does so when there is no pressure, he approaches moral leprosy. When he allows a subordinate to take the blame gratuitously for his own mistake, he is a moral leper.

Additionally, the boss is expected to try to get higher salaries and stock for his subordinates and to fight for them when they are criticized by the personnel of other departments. He does so because his subordinates are extensions of himself. He asserts his self-esteem by fighting for his "children." Not infrequently, though, the boss may think that there is a "fixed pool" of money available for raises in his department, or a fixed amount of stock available for such disposition. He can thus conceive of himself in competition with his subordinates. To get a larger share for himself, he denies benefits to his subordinates. The latter, if they find out, will conceive of the boss as a leper, and act accordingly.

A boss is allowed the pleasure of inventing "exercises" for his subordinates—hard, senseless work that keeps them on their toes and reminds them who is boss. However, this right is limited. He should rotate his "favors" among subordinates. Picking on one man is regarded as a sign of weakness rather than strength. Causing a subordinate to break down because of unnecessary exercises or pressure is a stigma of moral leprosy. In short, no matter how great the pressures placed on him, the boss is obligated not to increase the pressures on his subordinates just to make someone suffer as much as he does. This norm is more honored in its breach than in its acceptance. The boss who does honor the norm is viewed somewhat as a saint in Ivy League clothes.

ETHICS FOR SUBORDINATES WITH RESPECT TO THEIR BOSSES

The ethical norms for this situation come close to being work rules. Since the boss has means of enforcing the norms, the individual may comply simply in recognition of the power differentials involved. Yet advertising men do recognize some as ethical norms. These will be listed briefly:

1. Never denigrate your boss, even in situations where he has no chance of hearing about it.

2. Never take credit for your own work unless the boss has publicly acknowledged your contribution. After he has done so, one should modestly acknowledge the help, encouragement, and contribution of the boss.

3. Take the blame for the boss's mistakes if it won't get you fired.

4. Never go over the boss's head; don't squeal on him to *his* boss.

5. If you know that your boss disagrees with his boss or with the client but is afraid to express his disagreement, express the boss's arguments for him, even if you don't agree, so long as it doesn't get you fired.

6. Always show deference and respect for the boss in public situations.

7. In short, loyalty, deference, trustworthiness, reliability are all indispensable characteristics of the good subordinate.

ETHICAL NORMS APPLYING TO PEER RELATIONSHIPS

The norms that especially govern relationships between equals, or between individuals who are not in supersubordinate relationship, are essentially norms that define and regulate unfair competition.

The paramount norm of this order is *"Don't squeal to the boss about the derelictions of your peers."* The individual who squeals is a moral leper not only to the injured party but also to the boss and to anyone who discovers the talebearing. The reason is obvious. An individual who squeals against a peer is capable of squealing against a boss to the boss's boss, or against the agency to the client. Squealing is thus evidence of untrustworthiness. It also is indicative of an inability to handle oneself in competition. Only the man who is incapable of taking care of himself "runs to Papa."

Squealing thus indicates lack of manliness, lack of toughness, and lack of nerve.

The boss may encourage a subordinate who squeals to him. But if the subordinate does squeal, the boss may punish the party squealed against and distrust the "spy" who squealed. He is likely to inform the victim of the name of the informer, and perhaps encourage the growth of counter-informing. The boss who encourages subordinates to inform against one another is also considered by them to be morally leprous.

The norm against squealing is likely to cause a great deal of personal conflict and anxiety on the part of an individual who is aware of malfeasances committed by his peers. If he squeals, he is considered untrustworthy; if he does not, the malefactor can endanger himself, the account, the boss, or the agency. The individual must learn techniques whereby malfeasances can be brought to light without resort to squealing. He must arrange for the boss to discover the "crime" before it is too late. In the case of "too-lateness," he must pretend not to have known about the crime because, had he known, he could have helped prevent it at the cost of acquiring the stigma of being an informer.

The ethical norms against squealing and against losing one's temper substantially limit the techniques of interpersonal competition and rivalry. As we have indicated, advertising men are frequently in serious competition with all whom they work for and with, even though they are dependent upon those with whom they compete. The forms of competition are further circumscribed by norms against squealing, loss of temper, and direct appeals to authority. The solution to this problem is simple in theory and difficult in practice.

If there are to be competition, rivalry, and conflict between individuals, the norms "require" that all competitive activity be expressed in terms of the objective, stated, and public business of the agency. In appearance, this means doing a better job than a peer, or attempting to prove on objective grounds that the job one does is so good that all other jobs must, by implication, suffer in comparison.

One waits for or arranges an issue where one is diametrically opposed to the rival on objective grounds. One marshals one's facts, arguments, and supporters to one's offense or defense after the rival has committed himself irretrievably to his position. One impersonally, objectively, and without anger demolishes the rival's arguments and does this so conclusively that his nerve fails. If he concedes defeat, loses his temper, or is publicly embarrassed over a major issue, he may be forced to resign. The ultimate argument is that the rival's policy would result in the loss of an account, the inability to secure business, or the embarrassment of the agency before the client.

If the rival adopts this same line of attack against an individual, the latter can respond in a number of ways. He can refuse to become committed irretrievably to a position, and thus remain inaccessible to attack. Or he can have his defense, his arguments and facts, all prepared to meet the issue whenever it is pressed. The "likable fellow" attempts to avoid attack by never placing himself irretrievably in any position. He may succeed for a long time. He may take a position only after a stronger person, a "tough realist," has affirmed the same position. No individual can avoid taking a position indefinitely. This is the weakness of the "likable fellow." By not taking a position, he can be accused of neglecting his responsibility to the client. The client demands the best policy for his brand; having no policy is having a bad policy. If the "likable fellow" hides behind a "tough realist," he condemns himself to a subaltern's role. What is more, he is likely to be considered as not quite a "man," someone whom one does not have to reckon with.

Moreover, a "tough realist" can reverse himself suddenly, leaving the sycophant high and dry. When this happens, the "likable fellow" may find himself committed to an irretrievable issue.

The "tough realist" is a man who can recognize when an irretrievable issue is being raised, can foresee when to decline or accept the issue, and can carry his position through to a successful conclusion when he does accept such an issue. Fortunately for all parties concerned, such irretrievable issues do not occur too frequently, and when they do they can often be avoided.

Another ethical norm governs the ethics or perhaps the aesthetics of defeat. If one has been publicly humiliated, has lost one's nerve, or has been revealed as a "dangerous" person in a semipublic situation, one is done for. A person knows he is done for when other agency personnel begin to avoid him, when subordinates become less deferential or even argumentative or insolent, when peers begin to disagree with his most innocuous, agreeable statements, and when bosses begin to give him a continuous series of exercises or no work at all. The ethical thing to do in such a situation is to look for another job or, if necessary, to resign. By hanging around after having outlived one's usefulness, one reminds others that it could happen to them. One tempts others to self-destructive sympathy. One evokes guilt in the party who "necessarily" caused the defeat. One becomes an open sore in an organization that needs healthy defenses to stand the day-to-day pressures of work. Agencies are likely to give such a person plenty of time to find another job so that he does not have to appear as unemployed while looking for it. What is unethical in this situation is to force one's boss to fire one. When one does so, one forces the boss personally and falsely to bear the guilt of firing a man, when that act is actually due to the remorseless operation of the system.

One final ethical norm regulates the relationship between peers. This is related to the stealing of ideas. Ideas, plans, proposals, slogans, strategies are the basis of an agency's existence. Being fruitful is a major way toward success in an agency. It might, therefore, be expected that stealing ideas would be a major violation of advertising ethics. Yet stealing ideas is at most a minor vice. If an idea has been successfully stolen, it has been useful to boss, agency, or client. No one complains about a useless idea that has been stolen. Thus the boss, agency, executive, or client that accepts a stolen idea is pleased (at the moment of acceptance) with the idea. He is less concerned with the origins of the idea than with its utility. Moreover, the thief of an idea, to be successful, must first be able to sell the idea. The idea becomes an objective reality when it is "sold." Thus, originating an idea is less important than selling it. The originator is to be pitied only if he allowed someone else to steal and sell his idea. The thief is not to be blamed.

The originator may have a sense of personal injury at the thief, but the sense of loss is not transferred to higher levels so long as the agency gets credit for serving the client. When a man gets the reputation of stealing all his ideas, either from peers or outsiders, he is *not* considered to be a moral leper so long as he steals "good" ideas and sells them successfully. But he earns disapprobation on other grounds. A man who is forced to steal ideas obviously cannot create them. Stealing ideas thus is proof of lack of creativity, talent, and imagination. Such an evaluation of a man is made not on ethical grounds but on grounds of lack of ability. It is made primarily by his peers and not by his superiors. Superiors are concerned with results. A successful idea is a successful idea no matter where it originates, and one should perhaps not inquire too closely concerning sources.

CONCLUSION

The image we present of advertising is not a pleasant one. In some sense we have overdrawn the picture. Certainly the norms of not losing one's temper, and of competing in terms of public, objective, and functional purpose, mean that the public life of the agency does not appear unhealthy. Moreover, the relatively quick resignation of the "open sores" keeps the "unhealthy-looking" man from beclouding the sunny, optimistic, and constructive atmosphere of the agency.

In addition, it is difficult to be too critical of advertising because it is not so very different from most areas of upper-middle-class life. We have noted that advertising is different from other "executive suite" life only insofar as it distills and concentrates the essence of the executive suite. Advertising pays the same material rewards that are central to the American dream. The rewards are greater than can usually be found in other businesses, and are available to more individuals. It is perhaps only just that the risks—personal, professional, and psychological—are greater in advertising than in most other professions. If one wants to play for big stakes, one must be prepared to suffer big losses.

Moreover, simply because of the pressures, difficulties, and irrationalities that are central to its structure, advertising recruits, selects, and rewards those individuals who are psychologically attuned to its environment. In addition to material rewards, it offers deep-seated psychological rewards, a feeling of narcissistic well-being, to those who can meet the demands imposed on them by the nature of the work itself. It is unfortunate that many men discover only after having devoted half a career to advertising that they are not equipped to work in the field. This belated discovery occurs only because the demands and pressure placed upon a man increase with length of service and with responsibility. More-

over, failure in advertising is often more final than in other
professions.

One way to evaluate advertising as a career or a profession is to ask the questions "Would you recommend advertising as a career to the son of a dear friend?" and "Under
what conditions would you recommend it?"

The answer that this author would make constitutes his
summary of this essay. If the son has genuine talent or
creative ability in any field, advertising is the last place for
him to be. A truly autonomous, creative person will find
the pressures of committee politics and decision-making
destructive of his creative talent. If he accepts his new assignments, he must experience guilt for having betrayed his
original talent.

If the friend's son is kind, gentle, ethical, or religious,
and believes in spontaneous social relationships, advertising
would be an incompatible profession. Advertising requires
strong defenses, toughness, nerve, the willingness to exploit
oneself and others. Our young man might crack under the
pressure or, worse, develop these characteristics necessary for
occupational survival.

There are individuals for whom one could recommend
advertising as a profession. If a young man had no great
creative talent but was a good technician in an applicable
field, he might be a prospect one could recommend. If he
were fairly bright but had no talents, he might also be a
prospect. In addition, he would need a healthy constitution,
"nerve" but no nerves, and the capacity for hard but not
necessarily meaningful work. He would have to have the
capacity for handling himself, tact, and the ability to enjoy
superficial social relationships. He should be something of a
show-off who could control the need to show off and, in
doing so, be able to enjoy showing off to himself.

If he had all these qualities, and if monetary success or

the sense of power were sufficient motivations for his actions, he could be a successful and, perhaps, well-adjusted advertising man.

Obviously, advertising does attract the kind of men it needs to do a reasonably effective job of selling its clients' wares. In doing so, advertising as an industry fulfills the requirements placed upon it by other segments of the economy. Because it does so, it is difficult to say that advertising is better or worse than the society for which it is a cynosure. If advertising is to be condemned, much of our society is also to be condemned.

But as a place of work advertising leaves much to be desired. All work, but especially advertising, demands that the worker give much of his total personality, his total self, to the job. The very creative sources of a man are involved in what he gives to others through his work and what he receives from others by virtue of his work. The quality of one's work shapes, channels, and gives expression to one's creative energy. If the job demands the ability to exploit and manipulate others, both in personal and in impersonal relationships, the very self that provides the basic energy for these actions must of necessity be corroded by these actions. If one attempts to build walls against one's own exploitation and against attempted exploitation by others, a great deal of one's psychic energy is invested merely in self-protection. It is no wonder that the field is populated by would-be artists, novelists, scholars, and poets who rarely manage to fulfill the promise that gave meaning to their youth.

It is perhaps demanding too much to ask of people to give to their work that which in themselves they value most highly—in abstract terms, love, creativity, authenticity. But these demands cannot be made of the vast majority of employed persons in our essentially materialistic society, since the demands made by their work are somewhat less than

individuals at their best can give and, more often, are somewhat perverted versions of what individuals at their best
have to offer.

Advertising simply accepts the world as it is, and then
makes it even more so.

5

On the Pinnacles of Power—
The Business Executive

KENNETH UNDERWOOD

FOR ALMOST a decade I have been involved in an inquiry into the human and moral problems and tensions confronting executives or policy-makers in American business and government. This inquiry has been made chiefly with my initiative, but has deeply involved at many points scholars and students of social science, history, and theology, as well as social ethicists such as myself. Most of the participants have been members of the faculty of the Public Affairs Center of Wesleyan University, but scholars of Yale Divinity School and other neighboring educational institutions have also participated in this study of the nature of moral action in contemporary society.

The executives involved have been invited to spend varied lengths of time on our campus in conversations, study, and reflection, from a weekend to a year's "sabbatical." And part of the mutuality of this inquiry has been the opportunity for some of our faculty and students to be participant observers in business, governmental, and political organizations.

Out of this inquiry has emerged a beginning of a theoretical model of the human and moral problems that confront executive leaders in the major organizations of American life and of the way men think about their actions in meeting these problems. Our interest has been both in the way people think about their moral acts, and in the content and context of these acts. The executive does not separate what he is as a human being from what he does in meeting his responsibilities as an executive; our discussions with him move back and forth between his and others' understanding of himself and of his corporation, between the nature of the decision reached and the whole network of obligations and loyalties that set the context of and inform his actions.

Indeed, the central theme or concept that has informed our own research has been that of the social self, a concept that embraces our understanding of the subtle, complex, and continuing interaction of the person and the social structures of his existence. This is not a concept imposed on the modern executive; it is an expression of his human and moral situation; he is fundamentally concerned with the relation between the characteristics of the formal organization he administers or directs and the needs and characteristics of himself and of other human beings in it. The data of social sciences, social ethics, and theology that fascinate and involve him most deeply, we discover, are those indicating the way in which human beings shape organization and in which organization shapes human beings.

To state the data or findings this way is already to begin the process of selecting and appropriating the work of the university that is most real in terms of the world of the business executive as we have come to know him. For what he presumes in most of his own work, though he does not always articulate the premise or act on it, is that the human person, at least his own person, is not to be regarded as simply determined by and as a function of the organization, or that the organization can simply be viewed as reducible to persons. Self and society cannot be explained in terms simply of the other. It is the very nature of person and social structure that is at issue, a nature that has both its indicative and imperative dimensions, involving both what the person and the organization now are in their relationships and what they ought to become.

This view of the self and society has been worked out often by the executive as expressive of his own situation as leader, as policy-maker, as member of an aristocracy of talent and virtue. But the view has not been held as real for lower levels of the organization. And in this lies one of the major human and moral problems that will pervade this discussion. To what extent is the view of the social self being brought into consciousness by the executive something universal and human, and to what extent do the conditions and levels of work in modern organization produce a different relation of self and social structure (the executive assuming a "lower-level" self as infinitely manipulatable and plastic for the organizational purposes) ? How true or how necessary is this assumption for the achievement of the services and products that the organization is called into existence to supply?

The social sciences, ethics, and theology have developed many theories of the self and social structure that have seriously falsified and reduced the complex realities we are going to deal with here. But they have also often been highly perceptive, and more able to articulate precisely the realities of self, society, and God than the language of the businessman. We are, therefore, in a situation where we must with discriminating judgment move back and forth between the language of academe and the market in the description of the human and moral problems of the executive.

Indeed, this seems to bother the executive and the scholar less and less in our kind of society. What both are looking for is some relationship, at least once in a while, in which they can be really known in their work by someone who stands outside their situation, transcends it in a way, yet is concerned enough and involved enough to want to hear them out, to judge and evaluate them in terms of the possibilities in the concrete situations they confront. For a George Herbert Mead in American sociology or a Martin Buber in philosophical theology this is the way in which the self comes into existence. The self is not merely a natural or biological entity; it is profoundly social and moral. The self becomes an object to himself in his act of consciously imagining himself to be the other person; if the business executive commits the time and energy to hear himself and his work viewed by an economist, an ethicist, a theologian in the university, he may become more conscious of himself and the possibilities of meaningful action in his situation. But the scholar of the university does not help in this heightened self-consciousness on the part of the executive if he is unable or uninterested in an empathetic identification with the executive and his own organizational responsibilities.

What strikes the scholar, such as myself, who has sought to develop settings in the university to encourage this process of heightened self-consciousness is how difficult it is for all men, and particularly for men in highly complex and demanding responsibilities, to find situations in which they can be known and know others in this way, and how very threatening, often, are the discoveries of oneself and one's situation when such dialogue does take place. Our invitations to executives to make of their return to the liberal arts university an occasion of free, candid encounter is met both with an obvious desire to know oneself and one's work better through such experience, an awareness that one needs such heightened understanding, and a genuine fear and anxiety about such an experience. The return to business schools where the executive is more likely to be immersed in consideration of immediately recognizable management cases of decision-making are much less threatening than the consideration of philosophical, cultural, moral, historical, economic, political perspectives in one's life and work. The reading of "great books" and discussion of "big ideas" (such as the old American Telephone and Telegraph programs) is also much less threatening than the conscious appropriation of these liberal-arts disciplines for the reassessment of one's view as to the relation of oneself to the business organization he leads.

The executive I am going to use throughout this discussion as the "exemplar" or "representative" figure* involved himself very slowly and cautiously in our inquiries into his moral actions. (I have chosen one fictitious man and a fictitious company, and will stay with him so that the separate aspects of my theorizing will be seen as converging in or caught up in the life and work of a whole person.) Richard Bishop is president of a life insurance company with possibly $3 billion in assets, the National General Life Insurance Company. In his own words, he "dreaded our first conversation as to the moral and human dimensions of my work. I almost wrote you, when you indicated in your letter the subjects you wished to discuss, that I doubted that I could be of any help to you." In the first hour of our discussions he largely read statements that had been prepared by his public-relations staff in response to my comments and questions.

The interest our inquiries had in the relation of his

---

* Richard Bishop is of course a pseudonym, as is the National General Life Insurance Company. The profile of the individual called Bishop is a composite made up of data supplied by six individuals in comparable executive positions. This was done to protect the confidences of the people who were willing to discuss their work with us, but it does not affect the basic actions and views we are discussing.

religious background to his work were particularly a problem to him in our first association. He began with a report
on a "lifetime of activity in the Protestant Church. My
grandfather was one of the founders of the Baptist Church,
and I had three uncles who were Baptist ministers." But he
made clear that he was particularly "anxious to avoid getting
involved in discussions proving the morality or religiousness
of my work." Then he noted:

> I do not see the church as significantly influencing what I do and
> don't do in life. Its values and principles are engrained in one,
> but I never, when faced with a problem, consciously say to myself
> that I must adhere to or apply Christian principles. As a matter
> of fact one doesn't, as an executive in my judgment, separate or
> analyze one's decisions in terms of specific factors or areas such as
> moral or religious, that determine a decision. I just don't put into
> compartments my response to a problem in National General. If
> I did do this, I would soon become too self-conscious and rigid
> about my actions, too introspective to act at all.

A social ethicist can appreciate at once, with the help of
the existentialist literature and philosophy of the past century, the desire of Richard Bishop, the executive, to make
clear that the heart of his work is the decision, the free,
creative act, not reflection. The man of action appropriates
whatever he can from his past study and reflection and the
perspectives of his experts to meet a situation, to fathom the
alternatives of possible action, and then to act. The reflective
man is concerned primarily to analyze the factors that might
affect his acts, to weigh their importance, to try different
perspectives out on the situation. He will never be the
executive, the policy-maker. In this sense the academic
theoreticians and the executives are in tension. The executive cannot become so involved in the university or the
church that he becomes weighed down, made "rigid" was
Bishop's word, by the conflicting theories and perspectives
they offer on his situation. The varied perspectives must

remain the "precarious visions," partial and limited in their scope; the situation never can be reduced to the full ideological system. The executive moves beyond the relativism of these varied visions, and a leisurely reading of them in his stay at the university, to shape his situation in terms finally of his own *operational* absolutes.

A scholar such as myself tries to reassure the executive that he understands this fact about human action, while going beyond this initial resistance to too much self-consciousness. For the executive in time must and does go beyond a stance of intuitive mystique about his work. Richard Bishop talked on for three hours our first day together (canceling other appointments) about a whole range of policy acts that, as he described them, involved a vast complex of principles, images, values, technical data representing his own world view. And it was the role of the social ethicist, as I understood it, to help this executive clarify the operative perspective within which he made policy, and to be concerned also that his corporation might do good and be real. For what is at stake in so much of his tensions with other persons in his company is a fundamental disagreement as to the nature and function of the corporation, what is happening in the world—politically, culturally, economically, religiously, and so on—of significance to the company, and what are the demands and needs of persons in the organization.

Richard Bishop had indeed been brought to the presidency of National General because it was believed by the board of directors that he would be able to discern, from his perspective, developments in the life-insurance industry and the larger society that past offiers had not discerned, and would be able to make of these developments an occasion for constructive action in the company, and not for freezing into a defense of the status quo or for panic-crisis action that would bring the whole organization into turmoil and conflict. National General had, two decades before him, been a pioneer in life-insurance service and marketing, and ranked at the top of the industry in growth rate and assets. But its comparative position had grown steadily worse since then. Its executives had failed to respond to new merchandising methods of insurance (for example, the professionalization of agents, the use of mass retail store outlets) and to new forms of insurance service (for example, group insurance, inflation-adjusted policies, and so on). Its executives were talking less and less to one another about the realities of their situation; the attitudes of respect and deference toward senior executives had become stuffy and phony.

The responsible executive deals with tensions and change before they reach crisis proportions. Insofar as business, governmental, and other work organizations are functioning and viable in a society, they are led by executives who are able to discern and respond to pervasive changes in the world in such a way as to make them occasions rather than crises. Richard Bishop was able to help the leadership of his organization discern its occasions. When they could not, they were fired or moved from key roles. What was at stake, despite Bishop's restraining me from pressing for information as to his own world view being used, was the inadequacy of the perspective, the controlling images and principles, and the faith of many of the executives. They could not discern what was going on in the world and its significance for themselves and the company.

The basic question the university and church rightly ask of the executive in Mr. Bishop's situation is: What are the purposes and norms of your organization that are held in common not only by yourself but that are also operative for rank and file in meeting the conflicting pressures and demands upon them? They cannot do everything asked of them. They are a limited, incorporated organization, recognized in law with powers to hold property, sue and be sued, able to persist beyond the lives of its members, *and established for the accomplishment of certain purposes.* The perception by the executive of a juncture of circumstances and forces—an occasion—is made in terms of the particular purposes and powers of his organization. If the corporation is conceived as nothing but the organizational arm of its stockholders or policyholders, who are viewed as private property owners interested only in profit maximization and cost minimization, then political, cultural, and religious forces are likely to be held as irrelevant or as relevant in quite a different way than that of a corporation viewed as aiming at optimum profits and costs within a context of varied social and moral claims upon it.

The executive, then, as much as the academician, becomes involved in assessment of the vitality for persons in his organization of various loyalties and memories. What are the communities of interpretation for his executives: free enterprise, university, church, or what? And what are the dynamic images of their internal life that they draw upon for the definition of the firm's purposes? An executive such as Bishop sees his situation not merely as one in which he is an observer of something profoundly real and significant going on, but also as history in which he must ask what he and his organization ought to do to realize goods possible of actualization in the situation but not yet achieved. The policy-maker is concerned with what is actually happening in the world, what powers really direct it, and with what he and his organization ought to do in it. Policy-making is a way of responding to the world, and a projection of a positive pattern of action for an organization of men. The executive is to be understood as a person whose deepest moral influences are always related to programs; his faith is revealed in a pattern of positive commitments and decisions that he cannot (unless he steps down from his office) evade. The policy-maker provides the intelligence and character pertinent to the resolution of problematic situations into alternative courses and goals of action for his company.

It is little wonder then that he should, when he comes to the university to talk about his work, characterize it "as a way of life." In his first formal statement to our faculty and students, Bishop took as his theme a sentence on the opening page of a pamphlet his company uses in recruiting students for potential executive careers. The sentence says, "You will not be taking a job; rather you will be undertaking a 'way of life.'" Mr. Bishop then described what this way of life was for him in a paper he entitled "The Care and Feeding of Executives." The talk was a shock, and an initially repelling performance to most of the students and faculty. What they most remembered from it was Bishop's total commitment to an "eighty-hour week" in which one never "really separates his work and leisure"; the "Saturday executive training and study sessions at least once a month"; the detailed reports asked by his company of the interviewers of students who might be recruited into the firm: "Does he have clean-cut and regular features? Is he essentially a likable person? Does he have the ethical standards and personal habits required of a professional man? Would you enjoy a close association with him, e.g., on out-of-town engagements? Is he self-reliant? Does he have the courage of his convictions? Is he able to abstract and see interrelationships?" and so on.

What the talk did make clear was that the executive has an image of himself as engaged in actions that take the whole resources of the person. And this is the second aspect of the moral and human situation of the executive that I wish to note as fundamental and pervasive in American business. The young man who enters the modern corporation with career aspirations to reach executive heights may draw back from giving his whole life to the company—he has family and other associations he wishes to give himself to also—but he cannot draw back from the giving of himself, his full resources and being, to the work while he is engaged in it. This is what Bishop means by "loyalty" to the corporation and a "way of life." Before adolescent undergraduate students Bishop tried to make clear what it takes these days to master an executive position, to "ride herd," as he said, on a corporation. The whole being—mind, will, emotion—is called forth. Hence the probing of the interview into the whole fabric of a man's life, his way of thinking, his courage to act, his affections and habits.

He told the young men in utter candor if they wished to avoid the kind of "tensions which come with worry over the direction of a whole company, then plan your career for a lower level of work characterized not only by high technical specialization but also by simplification and impoverishment." The tensions of the executive are in great part those that accompany "higher mental syntheses" necessary to policy thinking. But the tension is also accompanied by a mental richness and psychic drive that goes to form the synthetic policy act. Bishop's language takes on at this point a conscious elite tone: "The narrow specialist has settled for, or is only capable of, a kind of gray mediocrity; he does not face the greatest challenges and the toughest problems in the society."

What Richard Bishop's view of his position reveals is the difference in his interpretation of the kind of character and personality required and developed at the "higher" and at the "lower" levels of the business structure. Work at the lowest levels of technical organization is designed by the policy-maker as routine and specialized in character. Each case to be dealt with at this level is reduced to its class. Rules and procedures are developed by the executive, not by the factory or office worker. The jobs at the "lower levels" are defined and evaluated by volume of work done, and such jobs are always vulnerable to replacement by the machine.

The factory worker is a feeder of a machine; the office worker is a digester of the input-output of the machines. The routine character of the work at these levels produces inevitably, then, in the eyes of Richard Bishop, a break between work and "free" time. Bishop, in response to faculty critiques, said he assumed that some alienation from work is always present in the office and factory. The new management literature he is familiar with (D. McGregory, *The Human Side of Enterprise;* James Worthy, *Big Business and Free Men*) is seeking to evolve patterns of authority that will decentralize responsibilities to some extent, open up more opportunities for workers to share in the formulation (or is it simply understanding?) of the goals of the company. But what Bishop wishes those who talk about a kind of "metrocorporation" to face is the limits and bounds to what work can be in modern technical organization. For decades to come, he argues, there will still be a distinction between the level of *obligatory* performance of routine work and the more creative and demanding work that the executive aspires to do.

The executive-manager is the one level of work the corporation permits general freedom from the desk and the time clock, because the nature of the work so deeply involves the whole person that he attends to it in all circumstances. His problem is that he can't get away from it enough to see it in perspective as not the whole of his life. The chief characteristic that marks him off in the society is that the major substance of his life is the life of the corporation. He takes the corporation into his home and the rest of his associations. His office is private, the way to him protected by banks of secretaries, for he must make the decisions of the company. To him are ascribed the executive virtues of imagination, drive, creative energy, intellectual and analytical powers, fairness.

The human and moral problems of this pervasive elite

culture are obvious. By what insight, by what relations to men who need to ascribe these virtues to him, does the executive maintain some capacity for human empathy for men and women in the "lower levels" of his organization, so that their desire to use their full powers in genuine service to others may be expressed in policy?

The policy-making executive is to be distinguished from the middle management-supervisor levels perhaps most basically in the excessively cognitive, abstract dimensions of his work. The manager directs the production and sale of certain goods within the conditions set for him by the executive. The manager does this with people he deals with on a day-to-day basis. The policy-making executive of the large corporation is dealing with men who are seeking to formulate strategy for a number of units of production and sales, establishing quotas and procedures that will fit into a larger whole. His thinking is necessarily more theoretical and intellectualized than the manager's, more removed from the interplay of persons in local institutions. The mind set he tends to develop is that of technical reason, always calculating the use to be made of persons and organizations to meet certain purposes. If he is an executive of one of the major American businesses, he goes at best once a month to see managers of each plant or store the corporation controls. He does not really get to know their situation in terms of the concrete pressures, moral dilemmas, heartaches, frustrations that go into the formal reports he reads from them. He always sees these people in relation to quantitative estimates he must make of their situation to fit the overall plans of the corporation. Technical reason is always defining a function or goal to be achieved by an organization, and then putting people to work meeting it. The human and moral problems for the executive come when men and women begin to ask in the organization whether this is a goal they really want to achieve, whether it is held in low esteem alongside other, more exciting, creative claims on their lives, whether they are capable of achieving the goal, whether they wish to fit into the role assigned them, or want the opportunity to refashion the role to meet needs of themselves and others more adequately.

However, an executive such as Richard Bishop finds it difficult to accept this picture of technical reason dominating his situation. He, like most executives who reflect with us on their work, is full of stories of personal acts of kindness for men and women with unique problems, as an expression of human compassion, even Christian love, in business. Bishop noted, for example, in one session of our faculty-executive discussions on the religious dimension of executive action:

I always seek to be sympathetic to the problems of specific persons in our company, and not simply deal with broad and long-term trends and movements. For example, one of our employees was scheduled to retire at a definite time; he agreed to this; it was in conformity with our company plan. He came to me and described the situation of his family, advising that his daughter had become seriously ill and that the required therapy was costing a great deal. To retire would reduce his income, and this would present real problems for his family from the standpoint of a chance for the cure of his daughter. If we wanted to be technical about this case, we could say: "Sorry, we would like to be helpful, but company policy must be strictly adhered to." Instead, we said that if an additional six months or a year of full-time work would help the family problem, we would work it out with him and then review the situation at the end of that time.

We try to deal fairly with people and to go as far as we can in understanding their needs and still have an efficient business; we take into consideration the varied problems confronting each person, and do not get bogged down in mass images of employee relations or needs.

Before the faculty at Wesleyan began a study in social ethics of the president of National General, a number of conversations were held with executives and managers serving under Mr. Bishop, in an effort to discover the human problems they faced in their relations with him. Several of these men were very concerned that we ask Mr. Bishop how he interpreted the nature of the resistance that many executives offered to his plans for changing the company. They still did not feel, even after they decided to accept the changes he wanted, that any profound or satisfactory reconciliation in their relations to him had taken place after hard-fought battles over the direction the "reform" of the company was to take. Therefore, after Bishop made the statement quoted above, one of our faculty made the following comment:

FACULTY MEMBER: None of us can fail to appreciate the difficulty an executive such as yourself faces in being responsive to the unique personal problems of your employees. You are always by nature of your office involved in setting precedents and norms by your acts. The responsibility to obey rules and to create new rules are both yours. I would think that you would have been confronted throughout your career at National General with even more difficult problems of human relations than this one you described, with executives who were not able to accept the very basic changes you were making in the company, and could not help but view your policies as personal threats to their status and respect in the company. No organization of men could have come through, as this company had, some basic changes in services offered the public and its way of making decisions without a tremendous cost in the lives of the men involved. The cost would be in part in terms of the anxieties, guilt and fears that would develop among men who felt their past way of operation was being challenged. These would be present perhaps not simply among men who had inadequate personal resources to work effectively in the emerging new organization but among men like yourself who were leaders of change.

I am not saying this very clearly, but even if your door was always open, as you say, and your colleagues came to talk to you about the changes proposed, could men like yourself really

know your colleagues well enough or overcome the limits imposed by your high position in the company so that these men
could speak to you in frankness of their criticisms, fears, and
aspirations? Or, to put this in theological terms, was there in
the men who led the reforms a sense of the finiteness and self-
centeredness which restricts men from fully understanding one
another? Was it possible to achieve genuine forgiveness in the
relations of executives, forgiveness as experienced perhaps in
one's family or talked about in the church?

BISHOP: I can't take the concept of forgiveness or any one facet
of moral or religious experience and say that this raises questions about what I said or did in a given case. Now, you were
not doing this. But you cannot criticize meaningfully a decision I make in business by introducing some religious or moral
principle and ask me if I adequately considered it in my action.
The principle may have entered into what I did but only in
my response to each situation and the specific people involved.

As you well know, it is never possible in any organization to
satisfy all the people. I am sure there are disturbed people in
National General, and some of their tensions may have developed from their evaluation of conditions in the company.
Of course, I realize that it is not always possible to determine
the origins and causes of such anxieties and fears.

Furthermore, there are some people who should not have
tried to make their career in a given organization. People with
limited backgrounds and inadequate education often spend
many years in an organization, yet in terms of responsibility
are relatively, position-wise, about where they were when they
started. The concern I have about such people is to see that as
few as possible are left standing in one place throughout their
careers.

A few of these improperly equipped people are in management. I think of one, for example, who is a very able technician
but as a handler of people is very weak. Thus far our best
efforts have not enabled him to overcome this limitation. This
will have to be considered in any discussion of further promo-
tions for this man.

Sometimes the hardest thing that you have to do for a man,
but the most responsible thing, is to tell him to seek something
else in the way of work. Forgiveness applied here as a univer-

sally good thing could lead one to do for a man what was not really in his best interest.

Yet I am quite aware that you can argue a decision both ways and that you can err in the judgments as to the potentialities of a man, for the people at the head of the company who have to make these decisions are just human too. They can't solve all the problems of other people, even if it appeared in the best interests of the other people and of the executives to try to do so. Such intent or claim would be too presumptuous.

When you try to know a man, you don't employ one factor in evaluating him, but you try to see him whole. You desire to see men develop their full potentialities, to get ahead, and you try to recognize people as people having problems, the same as you do. Now, so to relate oneself to another person, you can call simply good business, and it is, or you can call it love or the milk of human kindness.

I have quoted this very impressive statement by Richard Bishop to indicate the complexity and humility of this man's understanding of his own acts and of that of others. The business executive is driven by many forces in large-scale organization to an abstract and manipulative relation to his colleagues, but he may genuinely desire to go beyond this in his work. In the day-to-day problems of his own work he develops the ties of comfortable affection that come with the experience of men in community. Yet he also must judge and promote and demote these men in the development of an organization responsive to the changing needs of the society. Every word he speaks, every deed he does is watched and communicated formally or by the "grapevine" in a few hours throughout the organization. So he must play a public role with care, calculation, and compassion.

This leads me to the third basic problem of his moral and human situation as an executive, and that is its high dramaturgy. Richard Bishop is quite aware that he is involved in an often elaborate and subtle performance in the conduct of business. Much of his time and energy goes into the dramatic composition and theatrical representation of his position on problems on the company, and his office is in great part to be understood as a setting for his performance, his colleagues themselves cued almost by habit and instinct to keep the showing going.

The dramaturgy has to do, for example, with the manners and appearance of the president: the modulated, controlled voice, the cultivated sense of humor, the smile—now an automatic reflex when there is no amusement in what is said but once intended to set people at ease—the subdued dress; these are all part of the dramaturgy to convey the president's control over the situation, the reasonableness of his argument, the transcendence of personal invective and bitterness.

The problem with this dramaturgy is that though it has been introduced to control the relations of men so they can work out differences without acrimony, it becomes in time a means of hiding pervasive frustrations, despair, concern, controversy that need to come into the open as an expression of whole men who are creatures of feeling and emotion as well as reason, and as warnings that some things are wrong in the organization, that it is debasing or demeaning men, and not serving as an instrument of their basic hopes and needs. The problem of the executive, then, becomes one of taking part in a drama in such a way that he makes of business an expression of his deepest insights into himself and others but without making business the setting of his whole life and faith.

Richard Bishop often uses the image of his work as a "game" rather than as a drama, but the speculation of my colleagues in cultural history and in the arts is that his actions are more adequately viewed aesthetically as drama rather than as play. The work of the executive has its roots in serious material interests, but it sometimes develops play-forms as a secondary characteristic. A sporting element is sometimes introduced into commercial competition, as Johan Huizinga notes in *Homo Ludens,* when the drive among executives for the highest sales record, the biggest selection, the greatest speed and power, and so on, goes beyond utilitarian considerations. But on the lower levels, the introduction of such play spirit is viewed by workers and labor leaders simply as calculated devices to step up production or sales.

The images of drama suit the business world better, for the figures involved are less often engaged in activity just for the fun and intrinsic worth of it than in the management of roles developed and performed for the accomplishment of specific effects. The executive never wholly creates the role, writes the script, or directs the performance; he comes into an organization and culture that already has certain expectations of what a leader does. It is apparent that the more ramified, complex, and important the various specialties become in the modern organization, the more essential and elaborate becomes the dramaturgy of the executive. He cannot have the range of knowledge to know fully the basis on which various technical-expert demands are made of the organization, yet he is expected to be able to assign the problems to the right experts and to be able to coordinate the knowledge and values of them in policy. But the language by which he seeks to unify or integrate these technical specialties often has no meaning to the experts; the president can invoke no community of value by which men can agree to evaluate and coordinate the actions of one another. In this situation, a great discrepancy may develop between the projected self-image of the leaders and the realities. Dramaturgical skill becomes more and more coveted and prized by the executive and his associates as men play out roles that do not betray the lack of real agreement or common understanding in the organization. The tension in such performance mounts, for a reality always seems to be lurking behind the double-talk; the actors say one thing to one another, but mean something else. The audience becomes restless, sensing that the real drama of control and power in the organization is not going on where the more elaborate stage settings are present, but in the cluttered, half-finished offices of the technical experts.

Richard Bishop has been most reluctant, for example, to release for use in university courses any transcripts of our conversations that would clearly identify him and his company. When he asked the advice of his public-relations staff on the release of the material, the senior vice president of the public-relations staff told him that "the material does not support your image as president." And by this we learned that he meant that the discussion at several points moved into areas where the faculty was "aggressively" pressing Mr. Bishop for clarification of what were the principles or assumptions of his actions in difficult areas of investment policy, and so on, where it appeared that he did not have any explicit, meaningful (to the faculty at least) basis for the company's position.

In other relations with Mr. Bishop, it is obvious that he assumes our understanding of the highly conscious drama-turgical aspects of what he says and does. One of the more distasteful aspects of his dealings with church leaders, he once observed, was their "overseriousness about the relation of religion to business life." He gave an interview to a church magazine editor, for example, on his religious views and his activities in his own congregation. He gave him "what I thought he wanted, what would be good for church people to hear about the importance of religion in everyday life." He was disturbed when, after the article appeared, he received a number of letters from Christians saying that from now on they were going to buy insurance from National General because "a good, Christian church-leader was head of the company." This transfer of what is said in one role immediately to judgment of what is done in another role disturbed Bishop, even if it meant more business for his company. The problem of accountability and responsibility for the policies and "product-quality" of a corporation is in Bishop's mind too complex a phenomenon to be explained by one's church activity. In a burst of indignation against the churches' failure to sense the limits of his business life, he said, "I much more easily identify myself with Pontius Pilate, and the problems he faced, than with Jesus Christ."

It is to this question of the nature of accountability in the corporation that I now wish to turn, as the fourth aspect of the business executive's moral tensions and concern. The formal formulation of bureaucratic or administrative responsibility regards functions and duties as arranged in a hierarchy. The diagram of the office is a pyramid, with an ordered sequence of authority, each individual receiving his right to act from his superior and responsible to his superior for the manner in which he uses that right. He in turn delegates authority to his subordinates; authority comes from above, rather than below, and extends downward, defining functions and procedures (even to filing a given receipt) that will survive the death, departure, or promotion of the man or woman who fills it. In this monistic formulation, which has a great deal to be said for it as an insight into the conditions of modern work, there is a great dividing line between those who participate in the controlling decisions of the company and those who do not. No executive has full authority until he reaches the top, and then he may have been so used to passing on responsibility for determinative acts, he may not be able to exercise his *right* to formulate policy (that is, exercise his competency or jurisdiction), though he feels responsible in terms of moral *duty* or blameability. It is not hard to understand why within this system of authority the executive, once on top, so often relies upon the management consultant or the inside expert adviser.

Nor is it hard to understand the moral burden of guilt, remorse, and anxiety that often accompanies the executive office. The executive has the right to shape the organization, but he often finds the technical specialties so entrenched and incomprehensible, and the outside forces at work on the organization so faceless and formidable, that he does not seem able to act with effectiveness and clarity. He therefore tries to play down in public interpretation of his role the personal charismatic versions of his powers in favor of group process and egalitarian versions of corporate decisions. This also reduces his sense of guilt or blameability for the failures or evils of company action, for guilt or blame for the outcome of actions assumes ability to influence the outcome.

The statements of most business executives about their accountability for events in the corporation are usually highly ambiguous, diffusing responsibility over the "whole corporation," discounting the actual power to influence the market or the society, and stressing wide participation in discussion of alternative policies before adoption; at the same time, if the statements are read carefully, they do yield control of the organization to those to whom one listens. Talking about company policy to middle-management and worker levels is for their better understanding of policy, not their formulation of it.

Even Richard Bishop who was brought into faltering National General to ask the tough questions, to fire, to break through inertia of staffs, pictured himself in our initial discussion with him as working democratically to carry out committee-dictated, majority-voted decisions. The speeches written with and for him by his public-relations staff wallow in a sea of administrative jargon, which hides from view the inescapable responsibility for someone to move, to press, to order, to fight for what he wants a company to be at its best, to know the heartaches of defeat as well as the sweet smell of success, to be stirred enough by passion to sacrifice an easy, leisure-oriented life in order to give a large organization form and routine, purpose and meaning.

Here is some of Mr. Bishop's first statement to us about "accountability in National General":

The major policy decisions that a corporation such as ours arrives at are in the main the outcome of *group discussions*. For example, our decision to go into group insurance was considered and discussed for some time by the senior executives and finally the directors of the corporation. We had been historically one of the largest ordinary life companies in the world. It seemed to many of our men that we should stay in the area where we had gained our leadership. Why disturb ourselves? Others of us, as we looked ahead, felt that the company could render a greater measure of service, could grow and prosper, and improve its broad selling activity if it had both individual and group insurance in its portfolio. We realized that if we went into group insurance it would also mean getting into personal accident and sickness insurance, and that would require many new decisions. These are not all of the matters that were discussed before the company decided to move into the group-insurance field, but the decision was interpreted by persons like myself to be based on what was for the long run in the best interest of the company and its policyholders. This represents action emerging from many considerations and much group discussion.

As I look at my functions as president of the company and those of my executive colleagues, we are all managers or trustees of funds which belong not to us but to our more than 3 millions of policyholders. We have the responsibility to provide the various types of life insurance necessary to meet their contingencies and in the meantime to invest their funds as wisely as possible, so that we are in the strongest possible position to meet our obligations when these contingencies occur.

We are dealing with the savings of millions of people. I am impressed by the fact that in so many cases we are dealing with their major savings. So I have a feeling of real responsibility where so much is at stake in our policyholders' families. I must think in terms of our assets, which are over 3 billion dollars.

I have always made it clear that my office has an open door; that I can be seen readily. Now, I know that the persons in the lower echelons of the organization do not talk with me a great deal, and I understand this, but my executive associates do use the open door. Therefore, I believe that a claim to a successful atmosphere of constructive suggestion and freedom in the exchange of ideas has reality about it.

As you know, we have a field organization which represents our sales representatives. This group was developed so that our field organization could present its point of view to management. In meetings with this group we handle questions and suggestions in one of three ways:

1. There are some things that we can't do because of expense or for other reasons which we try to make clear.
2. There are some things which may be possible, so we take them under study.
3. There are some things which we know we can do something about, and we act accordingly.

This group could not function, and it would not be taken seriously in the organization, if our people did not believe that the executives respect the points of view of others.

We have a number of committees for the reason that we believe decisions on major questions are sounder if they come out of group discussion where associates can supplement and discuss each other's approach to a problem. Our committee and organizations, such as our field organization advisory group, are really important—because they enable a larger and larger number of people in the company to have a part in shaping the way the company operates.

Of course, some aspects of communication between employees and executives involve simply the giving of adequate information about the reasons for actions taken by the executives and the board. This is desirable in enlisting understanding and support for company policies.

Perhaps the dominant moral and human problem for a business executive such as Richard Bishop is that he works in an organization that must, if it is to fulfill its purposes in the society, operate with a hierarchical structure of authority in which those at the top can direct and control those persons on the lower levels, and yet he lives within a democratic society that puts great value on the egalitarian, voluntaristic aspects of human association. Mr. Bishop, like most leaders of large corporations, is searching for patterns of authority that introduce into this formal system some meaningful spread of responsibility and an atmosphere of openness to short-circuiting of procedures and form when creative ideas emerge from the lower levels. The impact of a purely formal, authoritarian structure is to make subordinate individuals dependent upon and submissive to their superiors. Individuals at lower levels do not have the technical data and liberating interpretation available at higher levels. Therefore, their concerns are most often for the tangible, short-run claims upon the company. Persons presumably developing toward mature and responsible action are required to work under conditions that require them to be immature.

What the business community may be facing in future years is something more basic than mere opportunity for discussion of persons on different levels of authority and for learning the reasoning behind executive action. The conflict and tension within the organizations may be not only about methods of achieving accepted objectives but also over the objectives themselves. The emergence of profit-sharing plans are one significant attempt to alter the objectives and functions of the corporation, which appears to influence the creative efforts of workers on the technical level. A work-leisure-oriented society has emerged in America, with the mass of people having financial resources and time now available for meaningful participation in all kinds of institutions and programs besides work. The American achievement of comparatively high level of affluency in the world leads to new mass preferences, such as for more "free time" and less productive work. These demands challenge the most basic values of the business culture. In future decades, work may not be the chief means of self-identity and self-esteem. Participation in voluntary activities, in politics (contributing to urban renewal, conservation, creative recreation), return to the university (for study and reflection, for development of new skills), the support of significant and demanding activity in the churches (adult education, social service), are all possibilities for more people than ever before in history.

And this occasion in the national culture poses the final significant moral and human problem for the business executive: Does he have the personal and corporate capacities to respond to these pervasive social changes in a way that reveals him to the people as a leader free to wander joyfully in this new world, able to cherish and sustain political, educational, and religious communications, as well as family institutions that are different from his business society and that, indeed, complement and at times correct and check his business activities for the justice and health of a greater society?

Richard Bishop has been both threatened and excited by this emerging new world. He wrote for a business journal recently a poignant and searching article in which he went through his appointment book for a "typical" day, showing that almost every item demanded decisions that could not be made without a serious consideration of government or political actions taken, or likely to be taken, affecting the future of his company—investment holdings in government bonds, apartment housing, a commercial center in an urban renewal program; Congressional banking committee "stirrings" over the "quasi-banking" powers of insurance companies; the effect of continuing increases in the cost of living on life-insurance purchases, and so on. At the end of the article, he noted:

That had been [his] day, and in its events he recognized the seeds of his discontent. Everything he had done that day, or not done, was neatly catalogued in his appointment book and had involved him in a way of doing things that was totally at odds with his deep-rooted system of values. He had always felt that managing a business effectively meant having enough knowledge of the factors affecting his decisions, and sufficient control over at least the critical factors, so that he could validly accept the responsibility for the consequences of his actions.

But this way of doing business had, he realized been progressively eroded by increasing government participation in the economy. The logic of events had made the government the greatest single influence, and very frequently the dominant one, in many aspects of his corporation. It was this fundamental conflict between values and circumstances, between responsibility and reality, which had for some time been lurking below the level of his consciousness.

Richard Bishop at the end of his article has his executive dictate a memorandum to his "Operating Committee." It proposed that "during our next few meetings we systematically examine the relationship of our company with the government." He proposed an "inventory of relationships between government and our company." He suggested the company seek answers to these questions: "How best to organize the company to deal with the government (are we too decentralized?) ; should we add to our information and control system? What policies do we want government to undertake to make us more profitable? What policies should we support to achieve objectives of national survival?"

In the article, the chief executive, having dictated this memorandum, went home "feeling he had accomplished something significant." But Richard Bishop's stopovers for discussion and reflection on these matters with our faculty revealed a continuing and profound perplexity as to how to move his company beyond the kind of week-to-week *ad hoc* decisions they seemed to be making in response to government policies.

National General has invested in two major urban re-development programs for "saving the heart of the city," but the commercial plazas they had financed already were pro-ducing side effects no one envisioned: for example, bitter relocation problems for minorities, the siphoning off of the more vital leadership from other areas of the city, caustic and telling criticism from cultural and artistic leaders about the monotony of the architecture and dominance of com-mercial values in urban planning.

Mr. Bishop's stay in our university produced some new sense of the cultural politics emerging in America that called for more attention to the human and social factors in gov-ernmental policies than his memorandum called for. But his stay at a liberal-arts institution also disappointed him in the lack of resources available in the scholarship of the faculty for opening up to persons like himself what criteria are to be applied to government and business planning for better urban communities, for economic and cultural de-velopment in new nations abroad. He is convinced that most business-school "advanced management study" is too nar-rowly pragmatic in the problems posed, but he discovered in the liberal-arts work few helpful leads as to the realities and possibilities of contemporary civic life.

His attitude toward the churches, as a source of insight or concern on such matters, is summed up in this exchange between myself and Mr. Bishop in a conversation a few months ago:

BISHOP: I just don't look at the church as an instrument for pro-viding major help in organizing or running my life. To me the church is essential as a representation of a deity, something higher and superior. It is an image of moral or ethical values I try to live by and with. It is a place I go to listen to a well-organized sermon which reminds me of divine reality, and to contemplate its meaning for an hour. The church has some social significance; this is why most of my friends are either Episcopalian or Presbyterian. It is the institution which marries you and buries you and you have to belong to it for these functions.

UNDERWOOD: You have told me that you read the *Harvard Business Review* pretty regularly. The *Review,* as you know, carries articles quite regularly on ethics and business, religion and business. Many of these come out of and use concepts or ideas about the nature of our contemporary situation which have been developed in the theological revival of which I spoke earlier. Are these articles meaningful and significant to you?

BISHOP: Let's see. Let's take a recent issue I have here, so we can be specific in answer. Now, here's an article in the January–February, 1960, issue I liked very much by Alvin Pitcher on "The Importance of Being Human." This is the kind of article you have in mind. Right?

UNDERWOOD: Yes.

BISHOP: Your comment about these articles is very interesting. I had not thought of them as coming out of the life of the church. I see here that Pitcher refers in the first page to Tillich and does throughout. I read it without thinking of it at all as an expression of a religious trend. I thought of it as a good description, as the editor says, of technological influence on society which is taking place all over the world regardless of ideology.

What intrigues me as I think about it is that this kind of literature never has been distributed to me by my local church. It is never discussed, yet as you say it is highly influenced by the thought of Christian scholars. I would never think of talking over Pitcher's article with people in my church but I will discuss it with friends in General Dynamics, for example.

UNDERWOOD: I think you have said some very significant things about the compartmentalized nature of your own church experience. When I read your article on world-thinking in business opeations I saw all sorts of theological and ethical implications which might come out in church discussions, were your article combined with the theological writings.

BISHOP: In many ways the church is in the same situation as the university in its relation to businessmen. Look at the influence the university has in the world, but business does not turn to the university for such influence. It reads the literature of the university occasionally, discusses it in its executive seminars, but chiefly as a tool to its own work.

The church and the university have a similar image to the public leader. They are places where one can get refreshment, but are not integral parts of what we do. They are seen by most of us as rendering a sort of fog which covers you, leaves you a bit dewy, but you soon dry out after the contact.

There is considerable evidence that business executives are making efforts to move out from a way of life which in past years has been dominated by the values and experiences of the business community into a new mode of relating themselves to other institutions in the society. These institutions will need to challenge their full powers, as does business, and speak to the actualities of a new society of which they are increasingly aware. The posttechnical society emerging could make possible a more personal mode of organization than we have had before in work and other major institutions. It could call out of the person a rich variety of powers and talents by his self-disciplined involvement in politics, education, and religion, as well as in business.

But, in turn, the policies the person would give of himself to achieve would be concerned not simply with the advancement of the profits of National General or "national survival," as Mr. Bishop's memo envisioned. They would be policies to enhance the whole institutional fabric of a pluralistic society. The education sought would have as its cultural hero neither the savant nor the technician, but the man of wisdom and social responsibility. And the faith made known in the churches would not be a vague image of "spiritual values," to use Mr. Bishop's phrases, but a radical monotheism, the source of the self's engagement with the world at large, the One in whom the many communities of one's life are made the instruments of social justice and personal reconciliation.

6

Some General Observations

on the Problem of Work

PETER L. BERGER

WORK IS one of the fundamental human categories. Man is the animal that fashioned tools and built a world. Man is thus the only animal that lives in two worlds, the natural one shared with all other inhabitants of the planet, and that other nature, a *nature artificielle* (as French anthropologists have called it), made by himself. Since it is this man-made second world that provides the context of any conduct properly to be recognized as human, the process by which at any rate the physical foundation of this world is constructed is of crucial human significance. This can be said quite apart from the question whether the symbolic edifice that necessarily overarches the human world should also be thought of as the result of work, mental work being then understood as a correlate or even derivative of physical work. To be human and to work appear as inextricably intertwined notions. To work means to modify the world as it is found. Only through such modification can the world be made into an arena for human conduct, human meanings, human society or, for that matter, human existence in any sense of the word. It is not surprising, then, that the great revolutions in the character of human work entailed transformations of human existence in its totality, from the so-called neolithic revolution on to the Industrial Revolution that is still transforming our own existence today. Nor is it surprising that work was imbued from earliest times with profound religious significance. If to work means to build a world, then it entails, in a religious perspective, a repetition or imitation of the divine acts by which the world was orignally built—and perhaps even a competition with these divine acts, as the myth of Prometheus suggests. To work is no light matter. To work is to mime creation itself.

Work as mimesis of the gods is a long shot from the questions that have been dealt with in this volume. In one way or another these questions have revolved around the problem of the meaning of work. It is, therefore, of some importance to see that this problem is a peculiarly modern one, related, as we shall indicate in a moment, to specific structural and ideological developments in modern Western history. In most previous societies the problem hardly existed in this form. On the one hand, work was a religious duty, on the other hand, suffering understood to be part of man's fate. Thus, for example, the Hebrew word *avodah* means "service"—both in the ordinary sense of work and in the religious sense of serving the divinity, that is, of worship. A similar combination of meanings probably underlies the Greek *leitourgia*. The Latin *labor,* on the other hand, means both work and toil, in the general sense of suffering. And the latter implication is borne out even more sharply in the Latin derivatives rendered by "travail" in English (French *travail,* Spanish *trabajo*), which probably come from the word *trepalium,* referring to an instrument of torture. There is little if any hint in all this of the questions we associate with work today.

To deal with "the problem of work," as this volume does, is to deal with peculiarly modern phenomena. The focus of the "problem" is the question of "meaning." Now, social phenomena are always "meaningful," but in most cases these meanings are taken for granted, organized in institutions, and fully legitimated in the symbolic system of the society. That is, "meaning" is not ordinarily a "problem." It *becomes* problematic as the result of specific transformations within the society, transformations that put in question the previous taken-for-granted institutionalizations and legitimations. It is, therefore, logical to ask what the transformations are that have made our particular "problem" possible. It seems to us that two developments are of decisive importance in this connection—structurally, the extreme intensification of the division of labor occasioned by the ongoing Industrial Revolution; ideologically, the secularization of the concept of vocation. We shall briefly look at these two developments.[1]

The division of labor is probably as old as human society itself, since the latter would hardly be possible without at least a measure of the former. With advances in the technology of labor, the division of labor naturally gained in complexity. The Industrial Revolution, however, with its proliferation of techniques and skills, led to an intensification in the division of labor unique in history. We are still in the midst of this process, with no sign of abatement, as Evan's reference to the growing listings of occupational titles in Chapter 3 of this volume nicely illustrates. Moreover, the Industrial Revolution has brought about an ever-increasing fragmentation of specific work processes, removing the worker further and further away from the product of his work. The classical case of this fragmentation is the assembly line, so well described in Chinoy's contribution. In the case of the automobile assembly line there is still knowledge, on the part of the worker, what the final product looks like. The present writer has known workers engaged in assembly-line work who did not even know what the product they were working on was actually designed for, except that it had something to do with parts of "precision machinery"—for all they knew, the workers might have been working on a part destined to set off a hydrogen bomb. Nor, may it be added, were they particularly interested in the question. This fragmentation of work has not remained restricted to the manufacturing process, but increasingly affects white-collar occupations as well. Large offices are set up on principles quite similar to those of the assembly line, and for the same reasons. Even some of the so-called professions have been subjected to the impact of these forces—there exist today situations of assembly-line medicine, assembly-line law, and even assembly-line scientific research, with physicians, lawyers, and scientists attached to a small fragment of the overall work process very much as the automobile worker is to "his" place in the assembly line. Work under such circumstances need not be hard or painful (that would be nothing new), but the question of its meaning is apt to become conscious much more so than in situations where the worker related to the work process until the final product emerged.

As the result of technological progress, moreover, there are constant changes in the social organization of work. Certain occupational specialties become obsolescent, others appear *de novo*. We are today very familiar with the crises brought on by occupational obsolescence due to automation, with such crises having become more and more central in recent labor/management disputes in industry. And it requires little imagination to grasp the human tragedies involved in this (though even this amount of imagination is often lacking in public annoyance with certain labor unions for clinging to "outdated" work rules—for while we have plenty of engineers to "update" the work, we have not been very successful in developing ways of dealing with the "outdated" workers). However, this is only part of the basic human problem, the external, or socioeconomic, part. But there is also an internal, or sociopsychological, part of the problem. Precisely because work has been for so long a fundamental human category, any particular work has been not only a means of livelihood but also a source of self-identification. To take a drastic example, the Hindu artisan who prays to his tools not only expresses the religious significance of his work but also, at the same time, essentially defines himself in terms of this work. To put it simply, for most of history men have *been* what they *did*. This did not have to mean that they particularly *liked* what they did—the problem of "job satisfaction" is as modern as that of the "meaning of work." To say "I am a peasant" was, very probably, a far cry from pride, enthusiasm, or even contentment. Nevertheless, it provided a self-identification for the individual that was stable, consistent, and so recognized both by others and by himself. To put it simply again, work provided the individual with a firm profile. This is no longer the case with most work in industrial society. To say "I am a railroad fireman" may be a source of pride, but the pride is as precarious as the occupational title. To say "I am an electroencephalograph technician" means nothing to most people to whom it is said. To say "I am an addressograph operator" means nothing for a different reason, not because people do not understand what kind of work it entails, but because it is next to impossible to derive any sort of self-identification from such an occupation, not even the self-identification with an oppressed proletariat that sustain many workers in earlier phases of industrialism. Fragmented and ever-changing work thus tends to become divorced from those social relationships and

events from which the individual derives his self-identification, and *ipso facto* begins to appear to him as problematic
if not downright meaningless.

One consequence of this has been the concentration of
the individual's search for meaning and identity in the so-
called private sphere, also a peculiarly modern phenomenon,
of which a little more in a moment. Another consequence,
though, has been a wild scramble for status among a large
number of occupations. Status and identity based on work
have become fluid, insecure, and thereby subject to manipulation. If one can no longer humanly identify with one's
work, in many cases, one can still "project an image" and, if
successful, reap from this various economic and social advantages. In other words, occupational status has become a subject of one-upmanship. Indeed, there are occupations that
can exist only by virtue of such one-upmanship. The hospital
orderly, whose lowly job in the hospital hierarchy includes
the removal of the repulsive debris of medical activity, may
describe himself as a "cuspidorologist" and perhaps even get
away with it, at least outside the hospital. What goes on
under the heading of "professionalization" in many instances
is not far away from this pathetic confidence trick. Occupations not only become obsolete, but long before this may
have to defend their reason of existence. Other occupations,
just emerging out of limbo and already aspiring to the status
of "professions," have to be even more strident in their
claims to life, respect, and a healthy slice of the economic
pudding. Thus the occupational scene today is filled with a
multitude of defense organizations and propaganda agencies,
totally bewildering to the average citizen and often enough
bewildering to the various official bodies called upon to li-
cence, adjudicate, and supervise in this jungle of competing
image projections. This situation not only raises questions
about such older concepts as that of "the dignity of work,"

but again evokes the specter of meaninglessness over the whole occupational scene.

One very important result of the Industrial Revolution, already alluded to, has been the crystallization of the so-called private sphere of life, a sociologically novel phenomenon located interstitially between the large public institutions.[2] Although this private sphere is, of course, dependent on the public institutions (especially the economic and political ones), it provides for the individual a decisive alternative source of self-identification and personal meaning. This has important sociological and social-psychological consequences that we cannot pursue here. What interests us is that this private sphere is, almost by definition, segregated from the sphere of work. Indeed, it was the industrialization of work in the first place that made possible the emergence of this new area of social life. The typical and statistically normal state of affairs in an industrial society is that people do not work where they carry on their private lives. The two spheres are geographically and socially separate. And since it is in the latter that people typically and normally locate their essential identities, one can say even more simply that they do not live where they work. "Real life" and one's "authentic self" are supposed to be centered in the private sphere. Life at work thus tends to take on the character of pseudo-reality and pseudo-identity: "I only work here, but if you want to know me as I really am, come to my home and meet my family." In terms of institutions, the most important process involved in all this has been the segregation of the family from the world of work, and its transformation from an economically productive to an economically consumptive agency. And, of course, it is the family that, for most people in our society, is the principal focus of private life.

This, as it were, ontological devaluation of the world of

work has had far-reaching consequences for its character, psychologically as well as morally. The old profile-giving capacity of work is replaced by a peculiar dichotomization of life. The private sphere, especially the family, becomes the expression of "who one really is." The sphere of work is conversely apprehended as the region in which one is "not really oneself," or, to use a social-scientific term increasingly and significantly used in common speech, one in which one "plays only a role." Lewis's account of the advertising man portrays this state of affairs most lucidly, but it may be found in the other chapters of this volume—with the possible exception of the one on the business executive, although the present writer is not sure but that Underwood's fictitious insurance tycoon may not have fallen victim to his own public-relations rhetoric at several points of his self-definition. If the individual apprehends himself in terms of a dual psychology, it is hardly surprising that he readily admits to a dual morality —as, indeed, even Underwood's type does quite openly. Private morality and public morality become quite different universes of discourse. One must beware here of quickly regarding this dual ethics in terms of "hypocrisy." Given the structural dichotomization referred to above, the dichotomization of ethical theory as well as moral practice is only "realistic," that is, appropriate to the prevailing social reality.

We would contend that this metamorphosis of work in industrial society has fundamentally changed its human character. In older societies one could usually distinguish between "noble" and "ignoble" work. While our business executive is undoubtedly engaged in work deemed "noble" by himself and by almost everyone else, and our apartment-building janitor is pretty firmly considered to do be doing "ignoble" work, the older simple distinction no longer holds in most cases. We would rather suggest a threefold division of work in terms of its human significance. First, there is work that still provides an occasion for primary self-identification and self-commitment of the individual—for his "fulfillment," if one prefers. *Thirdly,* there is work that is apprehended as a direct threat to self-identification, an indignity, an oppression. And secondly, between these two poles, is work that is *neither* fulfillment *nor* oppression, a sort of gray, neutral region in which one neither rejoices nor suffers, but with which one puts up with more or less grace for the sake of other things that are supposed to be more important—these other things being typically connected with one's private life. As in any typology, there may be difficulties in clearly assigning specific work situations or occupations in terms of it. But in most cases, we should think, the decision is not hard. In the first category, of course, are to be placed most so-called professions and the upper-echelon positions in the various bureucratic apparatuses. In the third category continue to remain many of the unskilled occupations "in the basement" of the industrial system. And in between, in the second category, is to be found the bulk of both white-collar and blue-collar work.

For better or for worse (and, by most possible criteria, probably for better), the first and the third category have shrunk in favor of the second. This would seem to be an inevitable consequence of ongoing industrialization. Rationalization of work, bureaucratization of the administrative machinery, mass organization for mass production and mass consumption—these functional necessities of the industrial system must inevitably lead to a shrinkage of the first category of work. Only at the top and in certain special positions elsewhere is there much room left for work that involves the totality of the person. More commonly the entrepreneur is replaced by the bureaucrat, the individualistic professional by a team, and the craftsman by a machine. But at the same time that the demand for masters shrinks, so does the demand for slaves. Work becomes safer and cleaner, its administration more humane, its demands in terms of time and energy more lenient. If some people have less joy in work, most have less pain. Whatever one may think of this balance of the human accounts, it will be clear that the expanding area in the middle will generate its own problems, different and perhaps less harrowing than those of a previous generation, but pressing nonetheless. And among these problems that of the "meaning" of work is central.

Our "problem of work" must, then, be understood within a specific historical and thus relative frame of reference, against the background of specific structural processes of modern industrial society. In addition, however, there is an ideological development to be taken into consideration, namely, the secularization of the concept of vocation. We cannot here give a presentation of the theory of Max Weber on this subject, and must limit ourselves to the observation that this theory is crucial to an understanding of the ideological dimension of work in modern society.[3] Weber showed convincingly how, especially through the agency of Protestantism, the medieval concept of religious vocation was transformed into the modern concept of secular work as a vocation, that is, as action requiring the individual's highest religious and ethical commitments. Even those critical of Weber's theory will concede that work in the beginnings of modern Western history has come to acquire a meaning quite different from the one it had in previous periods and in other civilizations—not only a religious duty to be faithfully performed, not only an activity endowed with weighty ethical pre- and pro-scriptions (such as, say, the *dharma* of Hindu caste)—but a "calling," in the sense of demanding from the individual a total and passionate commitment, channeling his entire life for the achievement of high goals and thus bestowing high meaning on this life. Needless to say, this attitude toward work must be seen in relation to the immense energy that modern Western man has invested in economic and technological activity, an energy (what Weber called the power of "inner-worldly asceticism") that lies at the main-spring of both modern capitalism and modern industrialism. Now, although few individuals today approach their vocation as a task undertaken "to the greater glory of God," the conception of work as the bearer of high ethical and personal meanings has persisted. In other words, the concept of vocation persists in a secularized form, maximally in the continued notion that work will provide the ultimate "fulfill-ment" of the individual's life, and minimally in the expectation that, in some shape or form, work will have some meaning for him personally.

If we now try to see the structural and the ideological developments together, we are confronted by a paradoxical and even ironic situation. The structural development, as we have tried to show, makes it more and more unlikely that the individual will be able to "realize himself" in his work, forces him to look for such "self-realization" elsewhere, changes work from the exercise of a "calling" to the playing of a "role." At the same time, there persists an ideology of work that continues to present the individual with the expectation that he find his work "meaningful" and that he find "satis-faction" in it, an ideology that is institutionalized in the educational system (for instance, "vocational counseling"), in the media of mass communication and, last but not least, in the various occupational and professional organizations. Contemporary society does little to prepare its members for "meaningless" if painless pursuits. Rather, it inculcates in them the generalized expectation of an ever-fuller realization of "meanings" in everything they do. It is unfortunate that this expectation must then be carried out into a world in which it has very little chance of being met. Indeed, on *a priori* sociological grounds, one may expect that the ideol-ogy of work will gradually adapt itself to its structural reality. Indeed, we would argue that the "privatism" discussed above constitutes, at least in part, precisely such an ideological adaptation. However, as long as the old ideological expectation persists, our "problem of work" will continue to be particularly sharp.

How has sociological thought dealt with our problem? Before looking at recent American contributions, we shall briefly consider the treatments of the subject by classical sociologists.

There can be little doubt that much of sociological thought concerning the subject of work to this day is heavily indebted to Karl Marx.[4] This is due not only to the influence of his economic theories, but perhaps even more so to his basic anthropological presuppositions, many of which (usually without awareness of the source) have come to be taken-for-granted assumptions of the various social sciences. Marxian anthropology is, indeed, grounded in its concept of work. Man is defined and has historically defined himself by work. Man is essentially the being that *produces*. He not only produces a world of his own, but, as he does this, he produces himself. Physical and mental work are inextricably connected in the process of human production. The tragedy of history, however, is that man has become alienated from his work, that is, the world that he has produced has become an autonomous and even hostile reality that confronts him as an alien thing. Alienation separates man from the products of his work, from his fellow men, and finally from himself. Under the conditions of alienated work, man works, not in order to fulfill himself (the anthropologically "correct" mode of working), but by necessity and in order to survive. This fact forms the basis of Marx's critique of capitalism. Evidently we cannot here discuss the merits and far-reaching implications of these presuppositions. We would emphasize only that the Marxian anthropological conception of man as the producing being, especially the being that produces a world (or, as American social scientists would prefer to say today, produces culture), is indispensable if we are to grasp the centrality of work in human existence. And this can be said even if we then proceed to reject Marx's application of this conception in his theories concerning modern capitalist society.

Many of Thorstein Veblen's ideas on work can be understood as a peculiarly American modification of Marx's conception.[5] Like Marx, Veblen presupposes that man is essentially ("instinctively") *homo faber* ("workman"). While Marx, however, analyzed the social consequences of the alienation of human work in terms of the opposition of exploiters and exploited, Veblen saw the opposition more as one between confidence men and their "marks"—definitely a shift with an American flavor! Early in history there appear those who manage "to live by their mouths," doing so on the backs of those who continue "to live by their hands." "Ownership" and "salesmanship" are the opposites of "workmanship." There are, then, occupations of industry and occupations of waste. Like Marx, Veblen was also interested in the social-psychological effects of modern work (the "discipline of the machine," as he called it). We would argue that, for our problem, Veblen does not add much that is important beyond the Marxian conception—except for the aspect of one-upmanship, without which much in the contemporary situation does not make sense.

To return to the classical sociologists of Europe, one of Emile Durkheim's main works, *On the Division of Labor in Society*, is concerned with our problem.[6] Durkheim agrees with Marx (who, incidentally, adopted the concept from Adam Smith and David Ricardo) that the division of labor is at least one of the principal agents of sociohistorical change. For Durkheim, the change is above all in the character of solidarity existing within society—from the "mechanical solidarity" of less complex societies, in which there is little room for individual differentiation, to the "organic solidarity" of complex societies with a highly differentiated division of labor, and consequently with highly differentiated social organization. The latter, however, also brings with it a more sinister possibility, that of anomie (as Durkheim calls it), which is a state in which individuals have lost their social rootage and feel abandoned in an alien world. Durkheim specifically applied this concept to work, along with other social phenomena, and speaks of "anomic work"—despite wide theoretical differences, a term certainly to be related to Marx's "alienated work." However, there is a strong note of bourgeois optimism in Durkheim's notions of this subject: The development of "organic solidarity" makes unnecessary the application of rigid force to sustain the social system, thus diminishing class conflict and anomie, including "anomic work."

Max Weber wrote one of his lesser works directly on industrial work in a manner much closer to contemporary American sociology than the aforementioned writers.[7] However, his most important perspectives on our problem are found mainly in his major work, *Wirtschaft und Gesellschaft*.[8] The central aspect here is that of rationalization, as Weber calls it—the global process in modern Western history that renders every part of the social system more and more rational in its organization, procedures, and thought. Weber's theory of bureaucracy, still the foundation of nearly all sociological work being done on this matter, is part of this overall conception of rationalization. Implicit here, though not elaborated by Weber, is a social-psychological phenomenon—the appearance of human types suited to participation in a highly rationalized social and economic system.

Marx, Durkheim, and Weber supply the bulk of the theoretical tools with which contemporary sociologists have approached the phenomenon of work, with Veblen serving mainly as an American mediator for the ideas of the first.

As far as extrasociological theoretical sources are concerned, these are probably to be sought mainly in the discipline of psychology, though we cannot pursue this question. If we now look briefly at more recent American developments in the sociological analysis of work, we must look at two special interests—industrial sociology and the sociology of occupations.

While American psychologists showed an interest in industry prior to World War I, American industrial sociology can probably be dated rather clearly from the famous experiments at the Western Electric plant at Hawthorne, Illinois, which were begun in the mid-1920's.[9] These experiments, designed to test all sorts of factors influencing workers' productivity, took a decided sociological turn with the discovery (it really was that!) of the importance of the informal social group for workers' productivity. The key figure in popularizing the Hawthorne findings and integrating them into a general theory of "human relations" in industry was Elton Mayo, an Australian industrial expert who later became a professor at the Harvard Business School.[10] Mayo succeeded above all in interesting management in the results of the new discipline, and ever since industrial sociology has worked in close cooperation with industrial management, especially that branch of the latter (which also developed into at least a semiacademic discipline itself) concerned with personnel administration. Later research at Hawthorne involved two other figures important in the development of the discipline, Fritz Roethlisberger and W. Lloyd Warner.[11] The focus of industrial sociology continued to be the one fixed by the Hawthorne discovery—the relationship between the informal social system created by the workers themselves and the managerially designed work organization. In view of this, it is not surprising that the discipline has been accused of management bias and of lending itself to the nefarious manipulation of workers.[12]

There would be no point in tracing further the history of this discipline, except to point to its enormous development since World War II into a major branch of the sociological enterprise both in this country and abroad.[13] Its methods have become sufficiently broad as to lend themselves to application beyond industrial work proper, as for example in the military and in bureaucratic organizations of various kinds.

The sociology of occupations has a rather different background. It stems from the so-called Chicago School of urban sociology, which, founded by Robert Park, flourished particularly in the 1920's and 1930's.[14] Park and his students were interested in every conceivable aspect of urban life. Studies of occupations were at first more or less a by-product of this omnivorous interest. At first, the Chicago sociologists were mainly interested in socially disreputable occupations (if such one can call them!), as, for instance, the hobo, the taxi-dance-hall girl, and the professional thief.[15] These studies, however, became models for a careful analysis of the social worlds built on the basis of an occupation. The turn toward an interest in more respectable occupations may probably be marked by a study of the railroader, published in 1940.[16] After this, indeed, the discipline can no longer be seen as part of the Chicago School.

Since World War II the sociology of occupations has burgeoned mainly under the leadership of Everett Hughes, who taught for many years at the University of Chicago, where he trained an entire generation of students in his approach to the world of work.[17] In the present volume, we would refer to Gold's eloquent testimony to Hughes' inspiration for this kind of inquiry. Publishing mainly in the *American Journal of Sociology,* Hughes and his group have by now given us a considerable number of monographs on a broad spectrum of occupations. Although the sociology of occupations has not attained the place of industrial sociology in the academic and research establishment (which is easily explained not only by its age but also by its lesser pragmatic applicability), it is today a respectable specialty for sociologists to go into, and is taught as such in several places.[18] Its chief emphasis can still be traced back to one of the presuppositions of Park and his school—that no human activity is too humble or too distasteful for the interest of the sociologist.

It is hardly necessary to point out that the preceding pages could not have had the purpose of serving as an adequate introduction to what is by now an impressive body of both theory and data. They will have been useful if the reader has become aware of the fact that the discussions in this volume have behind them an intellectual tradition of some length on which, explicitly and implicitly, they build. What we propose to do in the remaining pages of this commentary is to outline three aspects that, we think, ought to be stressed in any sociological analysis of work—the structural, the social-psychological, and the ideological. These aspects may serve to put the individual discussions of this volume into a broader frame of reference and, beyond this, may be useful in indicating a sociological approach to occupations not dealt with here at all.

Every occupation operates within specific social structures. These may be analyzed under two aspects—the macrosocial and the microsocial. That is, one may analyze the occupation in terms of its location within the larger society, its economic base, its social and political organization; one may also analyze the occupation in terms of the individual work situations that it engenders, each of which concretely constitutes, and all of which typically constitute, a small social system. We would contend that a comprehensive sociological study of work ought to include both the macrosocial and the microsocial aspects.

The macrosocial structure is a miniature world created by those who work together, or, more accurately, created by them within the circumstances of their work. As industrial sociologists have well shown, this world is only partly designed and controlled by those charged with its official management. Usually it is, at least in part, a "counterworld" created by those expected to work in the world as officially defined by management. Even work with very low status and rewards is capable of giving birth to such a world, supplying to its inhabitants at least that measure of satisfaction that almost any social group has to offer. Gold's discussion of the janitor's ingroup sociability gives us a vivid picture of this. Subjectively, the importance of this world often becomes conscious for the individual only when he is threatened with separation from it, as in cases of unemployment or retirement. From the vantage point of anomie, even work situations that previously were conceived of in terms of drudgery take on the warm glow of a world in which one belonged.

Work situations obviously differ immensely in terms of the social world they create. The five studies in this volume should make this clear. The janitor, the automobile worker, and the engineering technician work in a world dominated by physical objects and physical tasks. Human beings are grouped and interact around these—garbage cans, moving automobile bodies, a variety of machinery. The advertising man and the executive, by contrast, work in a world constructed almost totally out of speech and writing. Within each of these worlds there is a complex network of human relationships and status positions, in which the individual must find and maintain his place. This is true of the janitor as well as of the executive. Solidarities are formed, manipulated, and abandoned again—in the "nerve-racking business" of the apartment-building basement, around the assembly line, in the gambling atmosphere of the advertising agency. In Gold's account we find a fascinating picture of a cohesive

social world created around one of the most unedifying occupations to be had in our society—but with its own ethos and
with its own ethics. The world described by Chinoy has
within it the powerful solidarity-generating agency of the
labor union, but aside from this is a world of anonymity in
which social relationships of any sort are at a premium. The
work situation analyzed by Evan is, above all, marked by
frustrated and, it would seem, desperate strivings for status,
on the margin of another occupation (that of the engineer)
whose popular ethos in American culture must be especially
galling for the one condemned to watch it from outside. And
then we have the glamorous worlds described by Lewis and
Underwood, that of the advertising man as a latter-day *cor-
tigiano* and that of the executive as a latter-day *principe,*
with forms of power and glory as well as of terror that neither
Castiglione nor Machiavelli could have conceived. The literature in the field is full of accounts of occupation-based
social worlds greatly different again from the ones dealt with
here—to mention two particularly fascinating ones, the world
of the restaurant and the world of the hospital, each with
its "frontstage" and "backstage" areas (as Erving Goffman
has aptly called them), with its manipulations of customers
and patients by a hierarchically structured staff, each revolv-
ing around an Ubuesque figure of splendor at the top of the
status ladder—the chef and the doctor, respectively, in the
dazzling whiteness of their ceremonial garb.[19]

It would be tempting at this point to make some detailed
comparisons of such microsocial worlds, comparisons of
which, we feel, there are too few in the literature that has
had an understandable tendency to be monographic. Such
an attempt, however, would break the format of these general
observations. We rather ought to emphasize now the other
aspect to be analyzed in the structure of work, the macrosocial one. Occupations, or at any rate many of them, not
only engender numerous social situations in which indi-

viduals interact face to face; they also constitute large social systems, often highly organized, that engage in complex inter-action with other systems or subsystems in the overall society. While this macrosocial world is not identical with the vari-ous organizations that represent and administer it (for ex-ample, the world of medicine is larger than the sum total of medical organizations), the latter offer the best opportu-nity of studying its structure.

Here there is a broad number of sociological problems for analysis—the relationship of the occupational organiza-tion to the occupation as a whole (contrast, for instance, the A.M.A. and the A.A.U.P. in this respect!), the legal status of the occupational organization (as, for instance, in its licensing and supervision powers), the internal power struc-ture of the organization (which may vary widely, as, say, in different labor unions), and the power politics of the or-ganization in the larger society (in terms of lobbying, pub-licity, and so on). This aspect of the structure of work has been mainly studied in connection with unionism.[20] While this is obviously an important area of investigation, it does not do full justice to the field. The world of occupational organizations is one in which a Veblenesque vision of gi-gantic conmanship is almost a methodological imperative. This can perhaps be seen most easily in the phenomenon commonly called professionalization, that is, the state of affairs when an occupation is out to convince the public that it is now entitled to the status of the older respected pro-fessions (of which medicine and the law are the prototypes). Sociologists have drawn up very serious-looking lists of char-acteristics that would entitle an occupation to claim pro-fessional status for itself.[21] This may be a meritorious task, but we would maintain that one misses the social reality in question unless one grasps the fantastic bamboozling that goes on as these characteristics are acquired or, more accu-rately, manufactured. The most important of these professional characteristics are, by common consent, the possession of a distinct body of knowledge, transmitted under the auspices of the profession, and a professional ethic, supervised under the same auspices. The ethic is somewhat less of a problem. After all, most occupational groups function within a modicum of moral ground rules, for their own protection if not that of the public, and these rules can fairly easily be codified. The body of knowledge is where the difficulty enters. What, after all, is the body of knowledge that properly belongs to social work, undertaking, or public relations—to mention three groups with recent but all the more noisy claims to professional status? The general maxim here could be put as follows: "If a body of knowledge does not exist, it must be produced." It goes without saying that this task is not easy, especially if it involves the construction of a plausible curriculum for the training centers of the nascent profession.

The social-psychological aspect of work concerns above all what monastics call "formation," that is, the shaping of character in accordance with the demands of the vocation. To use a sociologically more respectable term, work involves processes of socialization. These may be either voluntary or involuntary. In some cases, the individual eagerly seeks to shape himself in accordance with the vocational demands; in others, he has no such desire, or at least has no consciousness of the process that is nevertheless taking place. This invidious quality of socialization is an essential social-psychological phenomenon that can be observed generally; its operation in the world of work is but one instance of many.[22] Incidentally, even where the "candidate" for this sort of socialization willingly submits to it, he can usually neither foresee nor imagine the full consequences that will follow.

Every type of work socializes, at least minimally, to the extent that its efficient performance has psychological requisites. Even the lowest category of unskilled and undemanding work makes minimal psychological demands, as for habits of punctuality and predictability of appearance. For instance, the job of night watchman may involve nothing except that its holder be present—but, then, it demands at any rate that his presence can be counted on regularly and at specific hours. As one ascends the occupational hierarchy, the psychological demands obviously increase, the socialization process becomes more complex, and wider sectors of the personality are touched upon. As a result, more distinctive psychological types are "formed." As we commented before, modern industrial work, in its broad middle strata, has little capacity to create stable "profiles." The capacity, however, intensifies as one ascends in the hierarchy. It is still very strong in certain of the professions. In the executive echelons of management it is carefully fostered as a matter of policy.[23]

It is important to stress that socialization occurs not only and not even primarily as the result of deliberate policies or programs. The most important socialization agency is the work situation itself, which willy-nilly brings into being a social-psychological milieu with practically unavoidable impact upon the individual. This does not mean that the milieu acts as a power that can in no way be resisted. But the important point is that even when it is resisted or when the individual thinks out compromises with it, the milieu exerts psychological pressure on the individual *as* he resists or compromises. Each work situation may, therefore, be understood as a social-psychological milieu, which the individual enters with his personality more or less widely open to its influence. This is true of the factory, the office, the executive suite, and the faculty club, though, of course, the social-psychological details will vary greatly from one to the other.

The social-psychological milieux of the five studies in this volume differ greatly. We would feel that only the top two occupations (business executive and advertising man) analyzed are susceptible to the production of recognizable human types, that is, recognizable as belonging to the occupation in question, at least by those in the know. Underwood's principal character is not likely to be taken for anything other than a business executive, though probably a higher degree of initiation would be required to recognize him as an insurance executive. The human beings inhabiting Lewis's expense-account jungle are fairly readily recognized as types by the general public. An engineering technician, however, merges into a much more general category of white-collar, lower-middle-echelon types. And an automobile worker, as a human type, could just as well be a garage mechanic, as a janitor could be a slightly jaded army NCO. Nor are we engaging here in arbitrary imputation from without. Underwood's executive knows and is even proud of the fact that his job requires a total commitment of all his human resources—he is a fully conscious candidate for the emotional agonies of *Executive Suite*. And Lewis's advertising men are just as conscious prospects for the conflicts of *The Man in the Gray Flannel Suit* and *The Road to Miltown*. On the other hand, Evan's engineering technicians know full well their lack of recognizability—indeed, this is one of their problems! Chinoy's automobile workers themselves complain of the anonymity of life on the line, and Gold's janitors bitterly speak of the nonrecognition accorded them by their tenants.

The social-psychological milieu of work is not usually a fixed entity, but it is subject to rapid change as a result of technological or administrative innovations. Witness, for instance, the social-psychological revolution that occurs with the introduction of speed-up or piecework procedures in a factory, or when individual secretaries in an office are "thrown" into a secretarial pool, or when college faculty members are regaled with a closed faculty housing project. In such cases, the entire social-psychological milieu can change overnight—friendships are destroyed, old solidarities are replaced by new ones, status is won or lost, powerful new mechanisms of gossip and intrigue are set in motion.

Generally speaking, socialization here means the shaping of an occupational self-image consistent with the demands of the work situation or of the occupation as a whole. This is complicated by the fact that these demands are not always unambiguous and that at times the individual is confronted with contradictory definitions of his occupational role. Such discrepant definitions may be generally distributed through a profession (for example, the discrepancy between "hard" and "soft" police officers). Or, there may be discrepant role definitions between practitioners and clientele (for example, between social workers set on "clarifying the inner conflicts" of their clients and the latter equally set on deriving economic advantages from the procedure). Further, there may be discrepancies in the way different echelons define the work situation and its social relationships (for instance, managerial "paternalism" versus workers' "contractualism").

One of the most interesting phenomena in the social psychology of work is what Erving Goffman has called "role distance."[24] This is found when individuals consciously play the occupational (or, for that matter, any other) role tongue-in-cheek, doing exactly what is expected of them, but, sometimes vehemently, maintaining an inner distance with respect to their role. In our volume this phenomenon is found most clearly in Lewis's material. It is closely associated with the attitude Goffman calls "working the system." It should be evident that, with the exception of the more psychopathically inclined, this balancing act exacts a considerable psychological toll.

We turn now to the third, the ideological aspect to be considered in a comprehensive analysis of work. Occupational ideologies obviously vary greatly both in sophistication and scope.[25] Some involve no more than a few simple propositions expressing the viewpoint of the occupation. Others

involve highly elaborate intellectual constructions, sometimes blossoming forth into a full-blown theory of society—
often enough one of grotesque distortions. For example, the
ideology (if it can even be called that) of the restaurant dish-
washer may consist of a few ethical norms, mainly designed
to protect himself against the ongoing oppression of all the
others in the restaurant hierarchy, and perhaps some sort of
inverted and grim pride in the fact that he is sticking it out
at one of the worst jobs imaginable. American physicians,
on the other hand, at least through their professional organization, have found it necessary to develop a whole theory
of free enterprise, government, and individual rights to serve
as the backdrop for their ideological propositions. We would
contend that, if only in a rudimentary form, occupational
ideologies are present in even very low-status types of work.
Minimally, the ideology will so interpret the occupation or
the particular work as to enhance its importance. Maximally,
the ideology will produce a definition of a broad segment or
perhaps even of all of the society in accordance with the
vested interests of the occupation. And in between these two
poles, of course, there can be found a great variety of less
extreme forms.

The material in this volume is quite rich in illustrations
of all these forms. Underwood's executive represents the
maximal pole very well. Whether one ought to take his ideological propositions as genuine expressions of his self-image
is a different question. (Underwood does, but the present
writer has some suspicions.) In any case, whether "sincere"
or not, the ideology contains a fully integrated and articu-
lated theory of business, and of the place of business in the
larger society. The ideology also contains what can only be
called an aristocratic ethos, with high moral imperatives in
terms of general social responsibility, public "dramaturgy,"
and concern for one's subordinates. It is very interesting to
see how this ideology serves to legitimate specific aspects

of the executive's position, making them seem not only necessary but right. The aristocratic ethos assumes that there are
special character traits, presumably inherent in certain individuals (only a few, to be sure!), that entitle them to the
exercise of executive power. This, needless to say, has always
been a feature of top-dog ideologies. More complex is the
ideological assumption that "human compassion" and even
"Christian love" are adequately taken care of through acts
of benevolence toward selected underlings. We would argue
that this individualistic conception of "compassion" can serve
very well to lighten the psychological burden incurred by
actions that, on a grand scale, may involve brutality toward
others (although we cannot say whether this would apply
to the case analyzed by Underwood). Perhaps the salient feature in this executive ideology is the beautiful nexus established between "good business" and "love or the milk of
human kindness." The nexus consists of the assertion that
both business and the individual require the development of
"full potentialities." Since individuals with less than "full
potentialities" are commonly liquidated in the operation of
the business system, their liquidation can thus be interpreted
in terms of "their own good." Little need be added about
the convenience of such an interpretation!

Gold's janitors well represent the minimal pole in terms
of occupational ideology. Their work, to be sure, is too dis-
agreeable to be interpreted in any but rather grim terms.
Nevertheless, the silver lining is stressed whenever possible—
for instance, in the notion that the janitor is "his own boss,"
a dubious proposition at best, but obviously self-enhancing
and frustration-assuaging. The daydreams concerning possible escapes from the basement universe into some haven
of middle-class security serve a similar function—for example,
in the preoccupation with various highly precarious possibilities of real-estate speculation. But perhaps the most touch-
ing ideological element in Gold's material is the janitor's

self-image as "guardian of the house." Here one is almost tempted to think of archetypal mythological motifs. The janitor defines himself in terms that go back in a straight line to the beneficent spirits and genii of the archaic household, the dingy boiler of a Chicago apartment building is transfigured in the vision of the flaming hearth—and so, for at least a dim moment of consciousness, is the janitor himself. This ideology, however, does not extend beyond the narrow confines of the microscopic world it is designed to legitimate. Beyond it, "they" rule—the more powerful, the more successful. In this concept of "them" we can see clearly the social near-infinity that separates the janitor from the executive—society as "their" domain for the one, society as the open horizon for "our" actions for the other. All the more interesting is the fact that both janitor and executive feel the need to develop ideological propositions that, at least in part, are based in illusion.

Between these poles the density (if one may use this term) of the occupational ideologies increases as one ascends the status hierarchy. Chinoy's material contains little mention of ideology, but we would suspect that his automobile workers are strongly under the influence of the general ideological viewpoints of organized labor, at least as far as their perception of the immediate work situation and its problems is concerned. Evan's engineering technicians, of course, live or would like to live in the world of middle-class professions. Their foremost ideological problem is how to make plausible to the public and perhaps to themselves that their occupation entitles them to this position. And Evan gives us some good indications of how they go about doing this. When we reach Lewis' advertising men, in the courts if not on the pinnacles of economic power, the ideology becomes predictably "thicker." Lewis gives us a particularly illuminating discussion of the discrepancy between the public and the private ideological complexes, the former closely following the chamber-of-commerce rhetoric of the business executive but believed in by almost nobody on Madison Avenue (except for the quite comic Ivy League types described by Lewis), the latter a concoction of irony and savage "realism" that at least gives the individual the gratifying if not altogether accurate notion that he is holding "the system" by its short hair. What is also very instructive in Lewis' analysis is the fate of ideological themes derived from earlier stages of economic development. We would point here to the strange operation of an old "workmanship" ethos in a kind of vacuum or the persistence of non-Machiavellian moral ideas in a truly Florentine world of mutual throatcutting. If one likes sociological terminology, one could further analyze the latter phenomena in terms of "cultural lag."

We would once more emphasize the aspect of distortion that is pretty much an indispensable part of an occupational ideology. This aspect offers many intriguing instances that call for more detailed analysis. The burlesque stripper who defines herself as an "artist" engages in such ideological distortion no more than the instructor in a freshman English class who sees himself as an "educator." The undertaker suggests that inexpensive funerals provided by cooperatives are un-American, and the psychotherapist believes that the practices of any group of psychotherapists other than his own are unscientific. Each academic discipline (sociology as much as any other) develops ideas by which its own little games are made to appear as exercises in man's eternal search for truth, while other people's intellectual pastimes (especially those that in any way compete with one's own) can be interpreted as unscholarly and unserious. And so on and so forth. The occupational world, perceived as the arena of all these conflicting and cacophonous claims to importance, finally takes on the character of a fantastic carnival, a Mad Hatter's party, a human comedy. And we would submit that only this perception will do full justice to it, even sociologically.

The preceding observations have, of necessity, been sketchy. They will have fulfilled their purpose if they have placed the individual studies of this volume in a wider context and if they have indicated some of the general problems calling for further sociological analysis.

Returning once more to the five characters depicted in this volume, each one is saying in his way what the lamplighter said in Antoine de Saint-Exupéry's *The Little Prince:* *"Je fais là un métier terrible!"* And it truly is "terrible business" for all of them, though it affects them in different ways. We would have to reject as grossly ideological indeed the harmonious picture in the old English hymn about "the rich man in his castle, the poor man in his hut." Nevertheless, we can derive some consolation from the common humanity that unites our janitor with our executive in this general enterprise of pretending to be what one is not.

NOTES

1. In these considerations I have been generally influenced by Max Weber's understanding of modern economic history. The discussion of the character of work in contemporary society is based on what is now a broad consensus in industrial and occupational sociology, though I have felt free to engage in some fairly broad speculations on the implications of this. For more specific references, see below.
2. I am indebted to Thomas Luckmann for clarification of the social-psychological significance of the private sphere.
3. Cf., especially, MAX WEBER, *The Protestant Ethic and the Spirit of Capitalism* (New York: Scribner's, 1958, paperback edition of Talcott Parsons' English translation).
4. Most important for Marx's fundamental understanding of work, probably more so even than *Capital,* are his early writings (that is, those written before *The Communist Manifesto* of 1848), and among these especially the so-called philosophical-economic manuscripts of 1844. These are difficult to obtain in adequate English translations. Cf. KARL MARX, *Die Fruehschriften* (Stuttgart: Kroener, 1953).
5. Cf., especially, *The Theory of the Leisure Class* (1899), *The Theory of Business Enterprise* (1904), and *The Instinct of Workmanship* (1914). The first of these is available in a paperback edition by Mentor Books (1953).
6. Published in 1893, published in an English translation in 1933 (The Macmillan Company).

7. *Zur Psychophysik der industriellen Arbeit* (1908–1909), which has not been translated.
8. Most of this is now available in English translations. Cf. MAX WEBER, *From Max Weber: Essays in Sociology* (New York: Oxford University Press, 1946, paperback edition by Galaxy Books, 1958); *ibid., The Theory of Social and Economic Organization* (New York: Oxford University Press, 1947).
9. For a good account of the Hawthorne findings, cf. GEORGE HOMANS, *The Human Group* (New York: Harcourt, Brace, 1950).
10. Cf., especially, ELTON MAYO, *The Human Problems of an Industrial Civilization* (New York: The Macmillan Company, 1933).
11. Cf. F. J. ROETHLISBERGER and W. J. DICKSON, *Management and the Worker* (Cambridge: Harvard University Press, 1939); W. LLOYD WARNER and J. O. LOW, *The Social System of the Modern Factory* (New Haven: Yale University Press, 1947).
12. Cf. LOREN BARITZ, *The Servants of Power* (Middletown: Wesleyan University Press, 1960).
13. For a good textbook of the discipline, cf. WILLIAM F. WHYTE, *Men at Work* (Homewood, Ill.: Richard D. Irwin, Inc., 1961).
14. On the Chicago School in general, cf. MAURICE STEIN, *The Eclipse of Community* (Princeton: Princeton University Press, 1960), pp. 13–46.
15. NELS ANDERSON, *The Hobo* (Chicago: University of Chicago Press, 1923); PAUL CRESSY, *The Taxi-Dance Hall* (Chicago: University of Chicago Press, 1932); EDWIN SUTHERLAND, *The Professional Thief* (Chicago: University of Chicago Press, 1937).
16. W. F. COTTRELL, *The Railroader* (Stanford: Stanford University Press, 1940).
17. Cf. EVERETT HUGHES, *Men and Their Work* (Glencoe, Ill.: The Free Press, 1958).
18. For two good overviews of the discipline, cf. EDWARD GROSS, *Work and Society* (New York: Crowell, 1958); SIGMUND NOSOW and WILLIAM FORM (eds.), *Man, Work, and Society* (New York: Basic Books, 1962).
19. Cf. W. F. WHYTE, *op. cit.,* pp. 125–135, for an analysis of the restaurant system; E. G. JACO (ed.), *Patients, Physicians and Illness* (Glencoe, Ill.: The Free Press, 1958), pp. 448–500, for several analyses of the hospital system. For the concepts of "frontstage" and "backstage" conduct, cf. ERVING GOFFMAN, *The Presentation of Self in Everyday Life* (Garden City, L.I.: Doubleday-Anchor, 1959), especially pp. 106–140.
20. Cf. JACK BARBASH, *The Practice of Unionism* (New York: Harper & Brothers, 1956).
21. Cf. A. M. CARR-SAUNDERS and P. A. WILSON, *The Professions* (New York: Oxford Clarendon Press, 1933).
22. Cf. HANS GERTH and C. WRIGHT MILLS, *Character and Social Structure* (New York: Harcourt, Brace, 1953), especially Part III.
23. On medical socialization, cf. JACO, *op. cit.,* pp. 288–350; on executive socialization, cf. WILLIAM H. WHYTE, JR., *The Organization Man* (Garden City, L.I.: Doubleday-Anchor, paperback edition), pp. 69–154.

24. On the concepts of "role distance" and "working the system," cf.
ERVING GOFFMAN, *Encounters* (Indianapolis: Bobbs-Merrill, 1961),
pp. 85–152; *ibid.*, *Asylums* (Garden City, L.I.: Doubleday-Anchor,
1961), pp. 171–320.
25. For an overview of occupational ideologies, cf. NOSOW and FORM,
op. cit., pp. 403–440. A model analysis is to be found in Francis Sutton
et al., *The American Business Creed* (Cambridge: Harvard University
Press, 1956).